Return Statements

Incitements

Series editors: Peg Birmingham, DePaul University and Dimitris Vardoulakis, University of Western Sydney

An incitement is a thought that leads to a further thought or an action that solicits a response, while also testing the limits of what is acceptable or lawful. The books in this series, by prominent, world class scholars, will highlight the political import of philosophy, showing how concepts can be translated into political praxis, and how praxis is inextricably linked to thinking.

Editorial Advisory Board

Étienne Balibar, Andrew Benjamin, Jay M. Bernstein, Rosi Braidotti, Wendy Brown, Judith Butler, Adriana Cavarero, Howard Caygill, Joan Copjec, Simon Critchley, Rebecca Comay, Costas Douzinas, Peter Fenves, Christopher Fynsk, Moira Gatens, Gregg Lambert, Leonard Lawlor, Genevieve Lloyd, Catherine Malabou, James Martel, Christoph Menke, Warren Montag, Michael Naas, Antonio Negri, Kelly Oliver, Paul Patton, Anson Rabinbach, Gerhard Richter, Martin Saar, Miguel Vatter, Gianni Vattimo, Santiago Zabala

Available

Return Statements: The Return of Religion in Contemporary Philosophy
By Gregg Lambert

The Refusal of Politics
By Laurent Dubreuil, translated by Cory Browning

Plastic Sovereignties: Agamben and the Politics of Aesthetics
By Arne De Boever

From Violence to Speaking Out
By Leonard Lawlor

Forthcoming

Agonistic Mourning: Counter-Memory and Feminist Political Dissidence in Post-Yugoslavia
By Athena Athanasiou

Return Statements

The Return of Religion in Contemporary Philosophy

Gregg Lambert

EDINBURGH
University Press

Edinburgh University Press is one of the leading university presses in the UK. We publish academic books and journals in our selected subject areas across the humanities and social sciences, combining cutting-edge scholarship with high editorial and production values to produce academic works of lasting importance. For more information visit our website: www.edinburghuniversitypress.com

Edinburgh University Press Ltd
The Tun - Holyrood Road, 12(2f) Jackson's Entry, Edinburgh EH8 8PJ

Typeset in Bembo
by R. J. Footring Ltd, Derby, UK, and
printed and bound in Wales by
Gomer Press, Ceredigion

A CIP record for this book is available from the British Library

ISBN 978 1 4744 1390 9 (hardback)
ISBN 978 1 4744 1392 3 (webready PDF)
ISBN 978 1 4744 1391 6 (paperback)
ISBN 978 1 4744 1393 0 (epub)

Contents

Acknowledgements

I wish to thank the following editors of the journals and collected volumes where previous versions of some of these statements appeared: Jeff Di Leo, Victor E. Taylor, Carl Raschke, Kevin Hart, Yvonne Sherwood, Jack Reynolds, Rosi Braidotti, Bolette Blaagaard, Eva Midden, Irving Goh, and Verena Conley. I also wish to acknowledge the original occasions and the organizers of public statements: Jeff Di Leo, who organized the original panel on the theme of "discouragement" for the 2005 meeting of the American Comparative Literature Association in State College, Pennsylvania, where I delivered the first return statement; Clayton Crockett, who organized the roundtable on the work of Jack Caputo for the 2003 meeting of the American Academy of Religion in Atlanta, Georgia, where I delivered the second return statement; Gail Hamner, who organized a panel on the Continental Philosophy of Religion for the 2002 meeting of the American Academy of Religion in Toronto, Ontario, where I delivered the third return statement; finally, Timothy Murray, Director of the Society for the Humanities at Cornell University, for inviting me in 2010 to deliver the sixth return statement on Derrida's "Faith and Knowledge."

I would also like to thank Timothy Campbell and Philip Goodchild for reviewing an earlier version of the manuscript, and for their ongoing faith and encouragement; and especially my friend and colleague, Jeffrey T. Nealon, who has witnessed all of the various seasons of life that have motivated these reflections, and who has served as the most faithful companion and occupant of the bar stool immediately to my right since 2001. Thank you, Jeff, for always "being there." Finally, I wish to acknowledge my former teachers, who have always inspired and challenged my thinking: Jacques Derrida, "my only teacher"; Jean-Luc Nancy, who first believed that the 1989 Loma Prieta earthquake was only the trembling of his own thought; and Herman Waetjen, who taught me everything I know about the early Christian communities.

I am grateful to Peg Birmingham and Dimitris Vardoulakis for their enthusiasm in including this title in their series, "Incitements," and to Carol Macdonald, commissioning editor at Edinburgh University Press, for her experience and professionalism. I would like to thank Sophie Chapple for her careful editorial assistance in preparing the final script, and Bresser-Chapple for compiling the index and final corrected proofs; Tim Clark, for not missing an iota; and Iris Van Der Tuin, who has been both a wellspring of affirmation and a veritable source of key quotations from the philosophy of Bergson.

In Memory of
Charles E. Winquist, 4 April 2002
(friend, human, "all too human")

Introduction: The Return Statement

Most books are written with a clear statement in mind, usually in the space of a few years, as if to emulate a thought that unfolds as a continuous and unbroken element. This book is not among them. Rather, it has been patiently assembled from a series of public lectures, articles, essays, and chapters either written or delivered over the first decade of the millennium, falling roughly between the spring of 2002 and fall of 2012, all of which address the internal logic of what I call "the return statement" in contemporary philosophy.

This logic has three distinct senses or levels. *On a first level*, most of the statements that follow were written in response to what had commonly been referred to as the "post-secular turn" in continental philosophy and contemporary theory, which had been unfolding in North America and the United Kingdom during this period, even though there is a tradition that dates to a much earlier period in French phenomenological circles, namely from the early 1980s. My critical response to this phenomenon was primarily motivated by a series of questions concerning its relationship to another sense of the post-secular turn that was taking place globally following 9/11. I wondered, for example, how these two returns of religion could be taking place in such

1

proximity to one another without being directly linked, like the same horizon viewed from opposing perspectives of the globe. From one perspective the horizon is viewed as evening, from another, as a new dawn.

Even more troubling was the fact that different senses of the term "religion" (from the Latin *religio*) were being ascribed to these dual horizons of the post-secular. According to the first horizon, the semantic and cultural meaning of religion was weakening and philosophically pacific (though not necessarily pacifist). However, from the second horizon – mostly ascribed to the Islamic world, even though other so-called "fundamentalisms" (or what Jean-Luc Nancy calls "integrisms") were also gaining popular support in both North America and Europe – a literal meaning was reattached to the term, as if religion in this sense was the most direct signification of the phenomena and could not, for that reason, undergo any possible metaphorical substitution as, for example, standing for "culture" or "belief-system." From the horizon of the morning of the next day, on the other hand, the weakening of the sense of religion opened up a number of new semantic possibilities for other terms like "community," "faith," "love," and "God." Thus, weakness was also presented as a method of striking out or crossing through the literal sense of the term: ~~religion~~, as if by means of this operation, the signifier remained legible, but liberated from its historical representatives and institutional apparatuses. Consequently, it became possible for one to proclaim one's faith without necessarily being religious, just as one could be a militant without proclaiming violence, or even become a fanatic without necessarily becoming a fundamentalist (as in the case of the philosophical fanaticism proclaimed by Badiou as a new-found "passion for the Universal" concerning the idea of

"Communism," albeit a communism without "community"). In many instances, however, the new terms offered to replace the literal inscription did not evoke any "bond," oath or allegiance; they required only the most abstract proclamations of faith, truth, love, community, and hope. Thus it seemed that the only mortal enemies were the literal and historical senses of each of these terms, senses which seemed to belong only to the other horizon, or to the evening of the last day that was now setting on the West.

In my earlier responses to these dual horizons of the return of religion, in the spring of 2002 – which also coincided with passing of my close friend and fellow traveler, the "death of God" theologian, Charles E. Winquist – I began to consciously interrogate some of the implicit assumptions underlying this discursive phenomenon and questioned the frequency of Christian themes that were beginning to circulate throughout the works of contemporary theorists and continental philosophers, including even self-proclaimed atheists such as Alain Badiou and Slavoj Žižek. At the center of my earliest interrogations was what I perceived as a "catholicized" appropriation of the later writings of Jacques Derrida on the questions of religion and faith, especially by the North American philosopher John Caputo, but which was also discernable in the writings of Jean-Luc Nancy on the "deconstruction of Christianism [sic]" from around the same period. My earlier debates with Caputo are well known, and were the subject of a public forum of the American Academy of Religion in 2003, which was published that year along with Caputo's somewhat cantankerous reply in *The Journal of Cultural and Religious Theory*, an online journal that I had co-founded with Winquist in 1999, along with the theologian Carl Rashke, as well as Winquist's former students,

Victor E. Taylor and Clayton Crockett.[1] However, I was more interested in exploring Derrida's own writings on the philosophy of Nancy which appeared in 2000 in *Le Toucher: Jean-Luc Nancy*, and this work, along with the earlier address "On Faith and Knowledge" from the 1994 conference on religion organized on the island of Capri by Gianni Vattimo, became the central focus of my efforts both to complicate an all too easy assimilation of Derrida's later writings to a "weak theology" (Caputo) and to overtly politicize Derrida's position(s) regarding what he himself referred to as "globalatinization." This series of early interventions constitutes the first five statements of this volume, which were written or delivered between 2002 and 2005.

In my earliest statements I was highly skeptical of the entire phenomenon of the "return to religion," and perhaps my personal views have softened and become more mitigated or "ecumenical" over time. Nevertheless, I was immediately suspicious of an implicit and yet almost universal rejection of a certain critical tradition of rationalism that was often referenced under the name of Voltaire in the writings of Caputo and Nancy – something that Derrida also signaled with some concern in his earlier response to the French "theological turn" – alongside the modern representatives of the "hermeneutics of suspicion" (basically, the unholy trinity of Marx-Nietzsche-Freud). Even more concerning was the rejection of the more radical and scientific traditions of Marxism, psychoanalysis, and many of the "anti-humanist" positions at the basis of the schools of continental philosophy that had become dominant in North America and elsewhere throughout the 1990s. For example, in Caputo's response to what is included here as the second return statement, I am accused of still being "stuck in reductionism … like the cynics of Old," especially "now that the

4

reductionist accounts of religion – of the sort we find in psycho-analysis, e.g. – have been laid to rest."[2] Of course, I could never imagine a careful reader of Derrida's writings ever making such a claim concerning "all the reductionist accounts of religion," but especially the phrase "of the sort we find in psychoanaly-sis," which could be directly refuted by many of Derrida's own claims concerning the continued importance of the psycho-analytic body of knowledge – yes, even Lacan – for the possible future(s) of deconstruction. These statements, along with others in Caputo's response, only confirmed my earlier suspicion that what this phenomenon portends may be, in fact, a return of an earlier set of Christian and humanist themes that pre-date the tradition outlined above. Whether this signaled a "new humanism," or merely the second-coming of what Heidegger had earlier defined as "the first humanism" (i.e., Roman imperial humanism), which "*presuppose[s]* the most universal 'essence' of the human being to be obvious," was, I thought, one possible interpretation of the underlying sense of "the return of religion," which, in the fifth statement, I address as a mitigated form of philosophical fundamentalism (i.e., foundationalism).[3]

In the sixth statement, I return to Derrida's crucial lecture on "Faith and Knowledge," and especially to the very rich and very dense discussion that takes place in the footnotes where Derrida remarks the absence of any original or "proper meaning" of the word "religion," which is actually derived from three different etymological sources. The first source is the Greek term *threskeia* (cult, ritual observance); the second, the ambiguous senses accorded to the Latin term *religio* (in one sense meaning "to have scruples" and in another more "Christian" sense of *religare*, meaning "bond or obligation"); finally, one finds a third source, referring to the Holy or the sacrosanct, from the Latin *sacer*, or the German *heilig* (also meaning "whole," "soundness in health," or in Derrida's reading, "immunity"). In his argument, Derrida implicitly links the neologism "globalatinization" to the Roman Catholic sense of *re-ligio* (as the power of binding, creating a sense of obligation, permanently fixing the subject to the site – i.e., in the Christian cult of death, the site of the crucifixion) and thus seems to agree with the earlier claim of both Benveniste as well as Heidegger that the strength of the "objective determination" of this sense of religion is bound to the Western institutions of the State-Form, in both its imperialist (or Roman) and expansionist–colonial and its modern Christian-democratic histories. Following this thesis, the question I raise is this: which of the three senses of religion above can be said to be "returning" in philosophy today?

On a second level of what I call the "return statement," in the latter part of the book I attempt to investigate the internal logic of the return statement itself in philosophical discourse and practice, in order to question why it has become a frequent function of our contemporary "theoretical revolutions." For example, the "theological and/or post-secular turn" can easily be seen to participate in a general logic that is often deployed as a discursive practice to mark a change of topic or theme, to announce a new program or position, and at the same time, in a performative manner, to eventuate the passage of a prior "discursive function," whether this assumes the form of a proper name, the region of an earlier problem or authority, or that of an entirely new "conceptual territory" (*away* from the past, *beyond* the present, *toward* the future, etc.). For anyone familiar with the cyclical history of contemporary theory and philosophy over the last half-century or so, I do not need to demonstrate the predominance of this function which has commanded, in the purely technical manner of an automaton, the engine of its revolutions. Consequently, even while the "return of religion" is proposed by its theoretical practitioners to name an historically unprecedented "event" (either announcing the end of a meta-physical enclosure of theological contents that were precipitously repressed by an Enlightenment rationality, or the reversal of the prejudices of a previous critical culture dominated by the values of scientism, positivism, nihilism, and anti-humanist sentiments), we should also acknowledge that, at least on a purely formal or discursive level, it performs exactly the same meaning as any number of other such statements that have both preceded and followed this event, whether we understand the meaning to refer indexically to a "change of paradigms," or as the inauguration of a new discourse.

Of course, in the tradition of contemporary continental philosophy, the return statement finds its image (if not its archetype, or even its primal scene) in Heidegger's philosophy, specifically the abandonment of the existential analytic of *Dasein* in favor of the pure temporality of the "event" (*Ereignis*) in the later writings, which has been a dominant *topoi* for almost every philosopher writing after Heidegger – including, I would say, Derrida, Deleuze, and Badiou. However, rather than employing the somewhat mythical narrative of the Heideggerian "turning" (*die Kehre*), in attempting to describe the logic of this "function" I have simply borrowed a term that belongs to a computer programming lexicon. According to this lexicon, a "return statement" causes an execution to leave the current subroutine and resume at the point in the code immediately after the subroutine was entered, known as a "return address." I understand the execution of a return statement in philosophical discourse to perform the same basic function: that of leaving a current subroutine that has determined a previous philosophical logic and grammar, which Foucault described as an element of signification formed by particular traits defined by a sudden and discontinuous rearrangement, as I will return to address in the conclusion.[4] Likewise, a return statement will often have the performative and discursive function not only of marking the entrance of a new problem or a new theme in philosophical grammar, but also as effecting a sudden re-arrangement of signification, discursive objects, and subjective and objective positions, thus marking the entry into a new subroutine (i.e., discursive practice). In this sense, the many returns that have been performed in contemporary theory often bear the same programmatic function and can be said to merely constitute different subroutines running within a larger philosophical logic (or circuit). Once the subroutine is entered, it takes a period of time before the program is run and a magical keystroke is executed that will take it back to the point immediately after the subroutine was entered. While a particular subroutine is running, of course, there are many others that will enter into the same subroutine, constituting different variations of the same subroutine running for an indeterminate duration. According to this description, therefore, the philosophical program identified with the "return of religion" would function according to the same logic as the various theoretical subroutines that are running today, such as Speculative Realism, Object-Oriented Ontology, Post-Humanism, New Materialism, "Non-Philosophy," and the Anthropocene. And yet, I wonder, what is the internal logic of the program itself and how does one know whether or not – but especially when – the particular subroutine we are currently engaged in through our thinking, reading, and in our writing and other productive activities will suddenly turnabout into a point of execution that will complete and exit the program, where we find ourselves in the position of a new return address?

Each of the following statements was made specifically in an effort to investigate a current subroutine in contemporary philosophy from the perspective of a dominant return statement, but without attempting to initiate a new subroutine, or, in Foucault's terms, a new "discursive function." Instead, in taking up a dominant return statement, whether the "return of religion," "the body," "community," or most recently, "Life itself," I perform in each case a radical *skepsis*, a "suspension of judgment," concerning the function of the return statement itself, neither serving the continuation of the current subroutine, nor the performative of a new thematic or discursive practice either. In this manner, that of a "countersignature," I intentionally draw upon the critical resources of a more archaic philosophical method that, as I will remark many times, has been suspiciously foreclosed from the contemporary program of philosophy. According to a radical skeptical method, moreover, any truth-claim that cannot be invested with absolute certainty must be radically suspended, often leading to the clichéd understanding of skepticism as the complete denial of all knowledge concerning things or states of affairs. On the contrary, given the richness and diversity of opinions and the complexity of the states of affairs themselves, the skeptical attitude leads only to the suspension of the necessity of "belief," thus laying out a philosophical image of a life without belief, which only leads to error, suffering, and death. In the final analysis, to live without belief means nothing less than to live without the necessity of a judgment of/concerning God. In this regard, it is interesting to note that the most popular philosophies today, as in the early Christian period, could be defined as "first philosophies," that

9

is, philosophies based on the conviction, for or against, of the existence of God as a first principle. (For example, the recent position espoused as "radical atheism" would still belong to this scholastic trend, since to deny something is still to give assent to its negation as a first principle of philosophy.) Of course, a radical skeptic will view the creation of any "system" of philosophy, or any so-called "metaphysics," as a probable source of "error" for future generations – a premise that has actually been proven over the last 2,000 years and thus can even be regarded with a degree of certainty. Perhaps we have entered a new period of metaphysics, or scholastic theology – a new "dark age." In response, as I argue in the first return statement, given the current state of affairs, in my view it was precisely a skeptical attitude that had to be resuscitated and rigorously performed in a more or less direct relationship to the geopolitical events that were occurring in the post-9/11 environment, including what Deleuze and Guattari already foresaw more than two decades earlier as "a total war against an unspecified and unknown enemy."[5]

Finally, *on a third level*, we find that the function of the return statement has a much larger and epochal significance in the sense that most contemporary philosophies can actually be understood to share the same basic return address, which is to depart from a post-Kantian tradition of critique and from the theory of the subject. One of the major shortcomings of the critical or deconstructive tradition of post-Kantian philosophy is to be found in the fact that the anticipated advent of a new ontology remains absent, and, on the other side, the actual discovery of new possibilities for subjectivity has been "through a glass darkly," according to the Pauline phrase. In other words, critical philosophies of this tradition have never fully been able to depart from a negative or deconstructive phase and, as a result, the future is posited as a static and essentially "empty form of time," often accompanied by a "radical subjectivist" image of the event itself as an indeterminate, unpredictable, and ungrounded (hence "radical") commencement of an entirely new ontological order.[6] And yet, with this claim I will question whether we have only supplanted the universal pretensions of the Kantian Subject with a progressive number of new non-anthropomorphic themes that still pertain to a program to "de-center" the metaphysics of the Western (human) subject that is already pre-programmed by this tradition of critique.

Perhaps even as a reflection of the above trend, we have also recently witnessed the emergence of a seemingly concerted effort to displace altogether – or, at least, to radically bracket – the phenomenological experience of the subject as the origin of philosophical representation, as if the existence of the subject itself constituted the final form of error that contemporary philosophy wants to place under erasure in reformulating a new concept of truth. In my view, however, it is this form of "error" that constitutes a common element of signification that appears behind all the different analytical positions that have been recently gathered together under the general thematic of post-humanism. I will return to address this in the conclusion, in relation to contemporary theories that take "Life itself" as their object, as opposed to a notion of "living" which may have all too precipitously been reduced to "bare life," even if to fashion a positive and more affirmative biopolitical notion of the classical subject. Consequently, it is for this reason as well that several earlier philosophies belonging to this post-Kantian tradition, especially deconstruction, were either deemed to no longer be adequate for the future aspirations of philosophy, or seen as an image of thinking trapped by negativity, the post-Kantian limitations of critique, the hermeneutics of suspicion, and especially of an essentially anti-humanist prejudice identified with a certain "Voltaire-like" attack on faith in optimism, human progress, and the belief that this is the best of all possible worlds.

For example, I found myself particularly drawn to a statement that appears in Jean-Luc Nancy's essay, "The Deconstruction of Christianism," that "No one can imagine today being confronted by a Voltaire-like philosopher, having at Christianity in acerbic tone – and doubtless not in the best Nietzschean style."[7] It is partly in direct response to this claim that many of my own statements intentionally adopt a "Voltaire-like acerbic tone," mixed with a bit of Swiftian satire, as if to say: Why is this so unimaginable today? Moreover, especially in the post-9/11 climate, but also significantly following the tsunami that struck the Indonesian coast three years later, it is significant that the name of Voltaire appeared with uncanny frequency (even though this name was reduced to a mere signifier). In my view, this raised the possibility that we were witnessing the reactivation – Foucault might call it a "retro-version" – of the crisis of faith in reason and the belief in human progress that followed the Lisbon earthquake of 1755 and became the basis for the major philosophical positions of Voltaire and Rousseau, and even one of the topical sources for Kant's theory of the sublime (the other, of course, being the terror of the French Revolution). In the history of the representation of the sublime, terrorism has often been compared to natural disasters, such as earthquakes or hurricanes, and the attacks on the twin towers on September 11, 2001, resuscitated this "poetics of disaster." In the wake of these geopolitical and natural disasters, as well as the rising tide of fundamentalist Islam in some of the poorest countries that have suffered from being excluded from the global expansion of market capitalism, understanding Derrida's own remarks on the phenomena he called "globalatinization" became critically important. This is why Derrida's essay, written ten years before these events, becomes the central focus of several of the statements that were delivered between spring 2002 and the fall of 2008 and thus constitute the first half of this volume.

Earlier I called attention to the common sense (*sensus communis*) that many contemporary theories seem to share about our need to depart from a certain post-Kantian tradition of philosophy – and especially, any philosophy that begins by presupposing the centrality of the Subject (i.e., of Reason, Language, Structure, Culture, or *Weltanschauung*). Of course, we might also notice that this need for departure, or an "exit strategy," has been a fundamental "gesture" (in Walter Benjamin's sense) defining both our experience and the philosophical concept of "Modernity." Therefore, the act of simply bracketing (or crossing through) the experience of the Subject as the starting point for the investigation of our knowledge of ourselves, the world of objects, and other forms of life does not cancel out the epistemological and formal structures in which this knowledge is embedded, including the institutions and the disciplines we continue to inhabit, or rather, which continue to inhabit us and condition our thoughts, feelings and actions before we can even begin to determine ourselves by leaping outside our closed circle of experience. In fact, it is this apparent and structural impasse of what Foucault simply called the "the pre-reflective Cogito" – the concepts of the unconscious and ideology being only two modern avatars of this figure – that has led to some of the most desperate attempts "to escape" this philosophical tradition altogether in ways that can be viewed both as highly speculative, creative, and experimental, and yet also as pragmatically oriented, thoroughly disciplinary minded, and thus as the most promising new sources for the renewal of philosophy in the contemporary moment. At the same time, however, the act of beginning a new subroutine in philosophy, as in the cases of "speculative realism" or "radical atheism," also runs the risk of simply declaring the problems of the previous traditions to be either outmoded or completely erroneous, even "dangerous," whether we are talking here about "subjective correlationism," the philosophy of Heidegger, the ethics of Foucault, the politics of Derrida, or the entire history of critique following Kant.

Of course, the urgent need "to escape" from the past that determines our modernity is a theme central to Foucault's last writings on the subject of the Enlightenment, which is why both the first and the last addresses are concerned with what Foucault himself defined as our critical *ethos*, that is, "the permanent reactivation of an attitude ... of a philosophical *ethos* that could be described as a permanent critique of our historical era."[8] In other words, many of the theories that today espouse a radical departure from the anthropocentric frame of the Subject, even by experimental and affirmative means, continue to define the current state of knowledge in a purely negative manner, and all express an urgent striving "to escape" – to find an "exit" or a "way out" – often through the privileged perspective of another form of life, another culture or ecology, or a non-anthropomorphic vision of the world. If the Kantian definition of the *Aufklärung* expressed this initial state of the present from which humanity needs to escape as "immaturity," there are a number of critical themes that belong to the tradition of Western humanism that can equally stand for this negative state, including colonialism, racism, sexism, "speciesism," and a host of other "fundamentalisms" (or "integrisms") in the postmodern formations of biopolitical life, human capital, and the global war on terror. Could the critical *ethos* expressed by our contemporary philosophical theories therefore actually be understood to participate in and to perform "the reactivation of an attitude" that pertains to our own particular Enlightenment, or, at least, to the current stage of "immaturity" that precedes it? As a corollary, it is also as a "reactivation" of a different *ethos* that draws upon a different set of critical resources (for example, those offered by pessimism, skepticism, and even cynicism) that my own return addresses should be understood as often ironic and not as the expression of a personal or merely subjectivist response. In other words, I ask, why should these traditions be suddenly and somewhat precipitously excluded from our contemporary philosophical arsenal, and, more importantly, at precisely this critical conjuncture of politics? Here, I reject the assertions that I am speaking merely from an outmoded practice of suspicion, an anti-humanist sentiment, or a now defunct rationalism – much less am I speaking out of cynicism – even though I am indeed keenly interested in what new critical resources the more ancient traditions of skepticism and cynicism have to offer today. In this regard, I might even agree with Fredric Jameson's most recent statement in "How Not to Historicize Theory" that "Cynical reason ... might very well pave the way for some ultimate awareness of collective self-interest as such."[9]

Recalling Foucault's own late comments on the Kantian notion of *Ausgang*, that is, the negative attitude to the present that orientates a manner of thinking and actually doing philosophy toward an exit point (which I have defined as "the return address"), I have taken the following remarks as prescient in determining our own "epochal significations." As Foucault cautions:

If we are not to settle for the affirmation of an empty dream of freedom, it seems to me that this historico-critical attitude must also be an experimental one. I mean that this work done at the limit of ourselves must, on the one hand, open up a realm of historical inquiry and, on the other, put itself to the test of reality, of contemporary reality, both to grasp the points where change is possible and desirable, and to determine the precise form this change should take. This means that the historical ontology of ourselves must turn away from all projects that claim to be global or radical. In fact we know from experience that the claim to escape from the system of contemporary reality so as to produce the overall programs of another society, of another way of thinking, another culture, another vision of the world, has led only to the return of the most dangerous traditions.[10]

In the same remarks, moreover, Foucault admonishes us to eschew a purely negative attitude of critique that is posed too simply in terms of an "inside-outside alternative" for example, which he calls in his own epoch "the blackmail of the Enlightenment."[11] In other words, in some cases, the return statements that mark an exit from a previous philosophical tradition are posed in too global and radical a manner that promises a new epochal signification. In most cases, as Foucault rightly observes, we remain caught up in the same cycle of a modernity defined by the qualities of rupture and discontinuity, where an affirmative belief in our liberation from the forces that bind us to the past, exposing us to new forces that promise our destination in the future, is often immediately followed by the formation of new counter-modernities, as occurred in the period of the early Baroque following the Renaissance.

Foucault himself saw this danger clearly, perhaps more clearly than any other recent philosopher or historian, which is why I continue to privilege his own trajectory of thinking, beginning with the final statement he made on the contemporary question of "Enlightenment" and ending by returning to his own reflections on the concept of Life, written shortly before his death in 1984. In fact, in the earlier essay, with which this volume begins, Foucault already foresaw the objection that his own solution to this epochal problem was, in the final analysis, only partial and local, and would not in the end reveal – i.e., "in their truth" – the more general structures that may very well remain unconscious and over which we have little control. In response to this objection, he offers two defenses: Firstly that we indeed may need to give up "our hope of ever acceding to a point of view that could give us access to any complete and definitive knowledge of what may constitute our historical limits." Second, both our limits and the possibility of moving beyond them are themselves determined in both theory and practice; "thus we are always in the position of beginning again."[12] In these statements we find the clearest expression of the "return address" that also functions as the moment of return and recommencement of *the act of thinking*. In other words, they represent the reactivation of a radical skeptical attitude by laying out two maxims for conducting a philosophical life. Perhaps it is for this reason, finally, that my own critical attitude will simply be an effort to remain at the limit, that is, at the frontiers of the present epoch, and simply to test the validity of each "return" against my own human, inevitably "all too human," experience of our shared contemporary reality.

8 August 2015
Amsterdam, The Netherlands

Notes

1 See http://www.jcrt.org/archives/01.1/index.shtml (accessed October 12, 2015).

2 Caputo, "Love Among the Deconstructibles," p. 37, at http://www.jcrt. org/archives/05.2/index.shtml (accessed October 12, 2015).

3 Heidegger, *Pathmarks*, pp. 243–247.

4 Foucault, *Dits et écrits*, vol. 2, p. 1585.

5 Deleuze and Guattari, *A Thousand Plateaus*, p. 422.

6 See Wiseman, *Beyond Positive Economics*, pp. 230ff: "The essence of the radical subjectivist position is that the future is not simply 'indeterminate', 'unknown,' but is 'nonexistent' or at the point of decision." Interestingly enough, this is a position espoused by neoliberal economists, but also by several contemporary philosophical theorists of "the event," especially Badiou and Žižek.

7 Nancy, *Dis-enclosure: The Deconstruction of Christianity*, p. 141.

8 Foucault, "What is Enlightenment?," p. 42.

9 Jameson, "How Not to Historicize Theory," p. 582.

10 Foucault, "What is Enlightenment?," p. 46.

11 Ibid.

12 Ibid., p. 47.

1

Sapere Aude?

Every now and then it is useful to survey the course one has taken to get from there to here – even if only to answer the question made famous by David Byrne, "well, how did I get here?"[1] Occasionally, we might turn around and take in the view in order to evaluate our progress. To achieve this, one usually needs what is commonly called a "landmark," one that is clearly visible in order for the vista of the route taken to emerge. At this moment, in response to the question of how we got here, I will choose as my landmark a small brief that was written a little over thirty years ago by Foucault, shortly before his death in 1984. This text has the advantage of having been visible to many readers at some point in the intervening period, which is why I have chosen it for my first return statement.

In fact, on this particular occasion in 1984 Foucault is engaged in very much the same exercise and chooses for his own landmark a remarkable little text written by Kant some 200 years earlier. So, we might imagine, from our current vantage point, that we are standing on this peak looking back at Foucault on some distant peak, who has his back to us and is looking back at Kant, who in turn is not perceivable to us from where we are now. Between Kant and us, so to speak, there is a vista that we have called modernity, even though we have only a theoretical knowledge of its entire expanse, parts of it are entirely hidden from us, and we depend in some ways on Foucault's description of that stretch of the road, among others.

Speaking of this first stretch or duration, the part we cannot see, how does Foucault describe it? I will limit my remarks to three observations on Foucault's 1984 reading of Kant, each observation followed by some reflections that might help us understand where we are today, especially with regard to what I will call, following Foucault, our contemporary critical *ethos*.

My *first observation* concerns the notion of the limit attitude (or what Foucault describes as the critical *ethos* of the Enlightenment). Firstly, the famous motto (*Wahlspruch*), *sapere aude*, must be understood as comprised of two voices: that of Kant, and that of Frederick II. (Foucault reminds us that Kant's little article was written for a newspaper, comprising an address before the public whose rhetorical occasion would have to be analyzed in terms of the emerging discourse of philosophical journalism, or what today we would call the discourse of the "public intellectual.") It is crucial to see that each voice addresses a different limit of critique, a limit of the critical attitude, or even a certain limit inscribed in terms of a public barrier or guardrail. Of course, the limit that the voice of Kant addresses is epistemological and can be translated as "Have the courage to know the limits of your knowledge." Or, as Foucault frames it, the famous freedom to think has less to do with what we undertake in the act of thinking, or critique, with more or less courage, than it does with the idea of ourselves and the limits of our knowledge, a limit that inaugurates the permanent critique of ourselves within the creation of our radical autonomy (as a Subject, a "people," or as a "Humanity"). Foucault will define this critical limit later on as the realization of ourselves as beings who are thoroughly determined historically, and thus who are also fatally conditioned as "subjects" by the Enlightenment, whether or not we assent to this historical conditioning. For Kant, of course, the idea of autonomy is founded upon on the autonomy of the subject of reason, on the sovereign autonomy of the Subject itself as an "end" – the end of Humanity, the end of History, the end of Modernity as a project that is brought into being at the end of the seventeenth century and is, in many ways, still unfinished and running its course. As to the second voice, that of Frederick II, what does it mean when it says *sapere aude.* Of course, it addresses the limit of the Political Sovereign itself, of the sovereignty of the monarch, which can only take place in certain limits that respect the place of the sovereign. This voice can be heard as saying: "Think, reason, as much as you like, but obey!" That is, thinking must respect its limits, which are inscribed in the subject's obedience to lawful authorities.

If the motto of the Enlightenment project was "have courage" (dare to know, or, alternatively, "dare to be wise!"), then perhaps can we understand the critical *ethos* or attitude that marks our contemporary present as one of profound discouragement – *be very afraid to think critically*? I would dare to venture that historical periods marked by an increase in utopian social thought, in lieu of the invention of concrete political practices, can be understood in some way as epochal manifestations of discouragement. Likewise, an abstract and bloodless affirmative declaration of "hope," or the language of philosophical eschatology and "negative community," of the community or the democracy "to come," are equally signs of discouragement and betray the continued presence of a fundamental maxim of traditional modernism – *"the people are still missing."* Following this modernist political tradition, and given the current geo-political context, I would read the contemporary prophecies concerning the coming of the "multitude" in Hardt and Negri's *Empire*, or of "absolute democracy" in Negri's other works, as in part a Leftist reaction to this feeling of discouragement, which is perhaps why the macro-political and supra-historical vision one often finds in contemporary Leftist discourse frequently assumes one of the oldest narrative forms – that of the epic. As we know, epics are written in times of discouragement and distress, in periods of diaspora. In the pages of his *Theological-Political Treatise,* Spinoza first argued that signs of prophecy must be understood as signs of confusion and passion, as the expression of "confused ideas" and not as the expression of reason. This returns us to Kant's original argument, the intention of which was to distinguish the sign of modernity from the kind of heraldic signs of prophecy concerning the future of a people who are still found to be missing, or the failure of a people who actually exist to live up to the ideals prescribed for their future. By contrast, the kind of sign that Kant wanted to extract as a warning belonged exclusively to the present, as a sign by which the present was clearly demarcated and stood against the entire volume of the past.

My *second observation* returns to the famous, but infamously misunderstood definition of the Enlightenment as freedom – I prefer the term "emancipation" – from the state of immaturity (*Unmündigkeit*). I do not have time to go into the difficulties surrounding the translation of this German word, except to say that its English rendering focuses its meaning on the psycho-logical sense of maturation from childhood to adulthood, and not upon the legal and political senses of maturity. For the sake of economy, I will simply refer to Garret Green's argument, in his "Modern Culture Comes of Age," where he underscores in the German usages of immaturity, as well as "tutor" or "guardian," the centrality of the "mouth" (*mund*) – "indicating that the underlying meaning of *Die Unmündigkeit* (the immature ones) is being unable to *speak* on one's own behalf."[2] After all, what is the legal definition of the child other than a subject who cannot speak for themselves in areas of civil, political, and juridical life, who is strictly dependent upon the representation of a legal guardian – who occupies, in other words, the sorry state of being "a minor"? Green immediately clarifies the wider associations of this sense of maturity as "the ability to speak for oneself": "for that purpose one has need of a *Vormund*, a legally sanctioned 'mouthpiece' to stand in front (*vor*) of him – or her – as an official spokesperson."[3] This would imply the presence of a representative function of some kind –that of a "State" or of a legal-juridical principle of self-representation that underlies the subject of emancipation, such as the subject of human rights. Needless to say, if we remove all the overtly Victorian, highly moralized and psychologized traits of immaturity in order to arrive at a purely legal, juridical (even political) definition of the subject as defined by the right to speech and to public reason, then what better counter-proof, even in Kant's own time, could there be than the existence of the colonized? It is not simply ironic that this definition of maturity squarely addresses Gayatri Spivak's question "Can the Subaltern Speak?," since it turns on the problems of acquiring a voice in matters of self-representation and of being represented by an "official spokesperson," which have been the fulcrum of debates concerning who is authorized to speak on behalf of the colonized, or even the formerly colonized. Consequently, according to Kant's own definition of self-representation, the history of colonialism and the colonial subject has emerged as the most flagrant contradiction and counter-proof to the discourse of Enlightenment. Of course, what I am saying here will be obvious to some, and has been said before by others, but it is sometimes good to go over things again, especially given our distance from Kant, and the growing distance between the eighteenth century and our own.

Moreover, this legal and juridical determination has been at the center of recent debates concerning the subject of theory, and particularly the theoretical basis of the various discourses of counter-modernity. Perhaps, for my purposes, the most useful, straightforward, and certainly the least "Eurocentric" determination of the term "theory" can be found, not in Aristotle – whose definition of *theoria* has little resonance with the epistemological function of the discourse that goes by name today (which is why I would propose that we abandon the Greek usage as having no relevance to its contemporary function) – but rather in an essay by Henry Louis Gates Jr. where, interestingly enough, he cites Wlad Godzich's preface to De Man's *Resistance to Theory* in defining theory as simply the legitimizing and discursive transformation of the seen into the spoken.[4] What is "spoken" must be understood by the encunciative value that is added to the "merely seen," which I could render here as what is perceived or experienced by a particular subject or group. In itself, what is seen or experienced by a particular subject does not automatically have this enunciative dimension; rather, it is the extra or supplemental and performative enunciation of a discourse that functions, in some way, in the position of an "official spokesperson" that gives its representation of what is seen a special valence that today we define as "political." Of course, what is reported as critically perceived or seen (in the form of theory) is what is precisely absent from the discourse of another official spokesperson, which usually represents the discourse of the official European Enlightenment. In other words, theory concerns the epistemological limit that is found in the European spokesperson, a limit that addresses an elision of the seen and the perceived that is revealed by the array of critical subjects who constitute the current discourses of counter-modernity.

At this point, I would simply suggest that the enunciative dimension that belongs to current discourses of counter-modernity (including post-colonial and minority discourse) is primarily epistemological and institutional before it becomes political or social. In other words, what is being addressed by, for example, the post-colonial subject are the epistemological limits that define what we can know in the contemporary university. The critical transformation of these limits of knowledge will lead, if successful, to a renovation of the knowledges and the subjects of authority that populate the contemporary institution of officially sanctioned knowledge. However, such a transformation of the institution of knowledge, and of the array of subjects who are legitimatized and authorized to profess their knowledge, does not directly result in the social and political transformation of the society itself. This is true simply because the position of the university in contemporary societies is always found to be once removed from any direct contact with or influence on social and political institutions. While it has often been argued that is by design, in order to preserve the famous "freedom to think," the downside of this indirect relationship is that there can never be any cause–effect relationship built into the emergence of new theoretical and epistemological advances, and new subjects of knowledge, particularly in the Humanities, which already suffers from intense social, political, and economic devaluation (perhaps even what Roland Barthes defined as "inoculation").[5]

25

This is the problem I have with the use of the term "political" to describe the value of our work by many in our profession today, since, simply put, any transformative effects are epistemological rather than social, concerning the limits of what we can know, rather than directly addressing the limits of our possible actions. In other words, I would risk saying, in the form of a motto – *Epistemology Before Politics.* Of course, I realize that this statement can immediately be contested on the basis of all the indirect and non-apparent linkages between theory and social formations, but I would argue that the real test would need to occur in the analytic work that makes these linkages concrete and self-evident rather than merely associative and promissory – otherwise, we should consider abandoning our current use of the term "political," along with the term "critical theory."

My *third observation* returns again to Foucault's definition of *Aufklärung* as an *Ausgang*, a "way out," an "exit," even though Horkheimer would qualify this statement with the following: "the absence of a predetermined way out is certainly no argument against a line of reasoning."[6] If today many lines of reasoning must inevitably respond to the belief that there indeed may be no way out of modernity, at least as the latter has been concomitantly understood to reach its apex in the systems of globalization, then the real critical attitude in the face of this "no exit" lies where a real resolution to the problems of modernity seem to be lacking. Consequently, in response to this predicament, more recently – but, then again, in fact not so recently, so let's just say since 1985 for historical accuracy – there has been a burgeoning interest in counter-modernity discourses, those that have been developed *on the periphery*, so to speak, of the European project of modernity, especially in view of the history of colonization where the image of an already prejudiced rationality has been revealed alongside systems of racism, torture and imprisonment, impoverishment, and the devastation of the environment. According to Agamben's thesis, this has resulted in the reduction of human life to "bare life" – even of the famous "humanity in Man" which was purportedly the meaning of *Menschlichkeit* – especially in spatial and economic regions outside and between the globalized ecumenon of developed and developing states, where entire populations can be understood as the by-products (or waste) of Universal Progress.

At the same time, it might be critical to note that, according to another famous thesis of Foucault, what could be called "the waste of human life" has become the central problem of "govern-mentality" (referring to the bureaucratic objects of statistical knowledge, demographic plotting, economic calculation, as well as reparative programs of social security and political and historical models of rehabilitation and repatriation, including even the subject of historical memory and collective acts of forgiveness for past sins visited upon whole populations and peoples by earlier incarnations of the nation-state). However, with respect to other regions of the globe, at most this "biopolitics" becomes merely the object of an ethical discourse, and a pretty abstract one at that, concerning the so-called "Other," or the "subaltern." Here, let me again underline the fact that Kant's usage of the term "Humanity" is, according to Foucault, rather ambiguous and could refer either to the multifarious diversity of the types of human species distributed across the globe, or to the essence of the humanity in Man, which historically has taken the form of a particular Christian determination that has become associated with the derogative usages of "humanism" and "essentialism."

Nevertheless, I would say that we might glimpse in the privilege accorded to the subject of counter-modernity discourses the new image of "a way out" of modernity, or at least of an alternative discourse, which necessarily becomes multiple and open-ended, posing as a finite or partial solution to the historical dilemma we have outlined above – that of being historical beings determined by the Enlightenment itself, that is, by the character of "autonomy" that should be accorded to the political and cultural representations of a sovereign people to choose the principles by which they are governed or by which they supposedly govern themselves. In other words, if the strange double-bind of the Enlightenment principle of "self-legislative reason" has emerged predominately from the former colonized regions as precisely the contradiction of (or state of exception to) the Kantian precept of "self-government," this is not accidental, but rather I would suggest, is the necessary consequence of the principle of freedom first outlined by Kant. After all, is not the historical position of "the colonized" the most direct contradiction to the universal application of the Enlightenment principle of emancipated reason, which would also raise the question of whether our original interest in the colonized subject is really motivated by ethical concern, or whether it is the structural effect of a blatant contradiction in our own discourse of political emancipation? Here, of course, I am employing the term "our discourse" to signal the Eurocentric discourse of the Enlightenment project, even though this is a designation I have little respect for because I consider it to be an overused rhetorical strategy of current counter-modernity discourses.

For example, in the final part of Foucault's text, where he evaluates the critical relation to the Enlightenment in both negative and positive terms, he speaks "negatively" of the "blackmail of the Enlightenment."[7] This phrase has not been very well understood, since what Foucault actually means by this is a certain critical attitude commonly associated with the postmodern ideology of "anti-humanism," which often comes down in the final analysis to the simplistic alternative of being either for or against the Enlightenment. Consequently, in cases where the Enlightenment has already been defined exclusively in negative terms, who would ever be "for it"? Answer: only a creep, a real *bastardo!* This underlines the element of blackmail that Foucault was addressing in the polemics of his own time, which can certainly be applied to our own as well, and whose real effects can assume a form of censorship in certain institutional and public situations. As Foucault cautions, "the permanent critique of ourselves has to always avoid the too facile confusions between humanism and the Enlightenment."[8] I wonder therefore if we can speak of a similar confusion, perhaps even a modulation of the same one, but one which belongs to the current discourses of counter-modernity, including certain dominant traditions of post-colonial and globalization critique. There is now even a new form of blackmail, which I would call "the blackmail of Eurocentrism." In fact, is not the term "Eurocentrism" just another way of saying "Enlightenment" today, but with an already implicit derogatory value? In other words, the performative uses of this term have become too facile, and the same caution that Foucault outlined can be applied here in the sense that the term "Eurocentrism" is sometimes employed as shorthand for a set of critical prejudices that are directed against a historical tradition of European humanism – that is, as Foucault defines it, against a theme or set of themes that have historically emerged in European societies and were used in the arsenal of colonial ideologies (such as civilization, humanity, progress, history, culture, etc.). Of course, today this term has grown to have many meanings, most of them pejoratively employed to impeach a line of argumentation, of reasoning, a tradition of historical thought, a historical body of knowledge, or any mention of this or that author or critic who belongs to any (or all) of the above. However, the element of blackmail is often evident in the most common usage, echoing Foucault's earlier observation on the blackmail of the Enlightenment: "either you are for or against" what is proposed with a certain authority as running counter to the traditions outlined above. I would venture to suggest that the usage of this term is approaching an absolutely negative sense of wholesale rejection of everything that engages this tradition, even critically, and that one can often witness this usage in hiring committees or in editorial juries where a certain candidacy or line of argumentation is casually dismissed on the sole criterion of this judgment. Today, I worry about the seductive power this authority represents, particularly for those young intellectuals who still lack the maturity to speak *for* themselves. As they say, "authority corrupts," but most of all I am concerned about the blackmail character which has proven to function as a new form of censorship of thinking, as younger intellectuals and academics are coerced by the prohibition that this term represents to avoid entering into any engagement, even in a dismissive or second-hand manner, with the traditions that have historically determined the subject of their thought, and for this reason might be condemning themselves to remain in a state of permanent intellectual immaturity (i.e., childhood).

My real problem with this negative and facile usage, however, aside from a certain unreflective prejudice it represents and often reproduces institutionally, across the generations, is that it fails to grasp the term's positive and "political" meaning. In other words, critically and positively understood, the term "Eurocentrism" expresses nothing more than *the current stage of "our Enlightenment"* or, as Foucault defined it, "the permanent critique of ourselves in the creation of our autonomy."[9] Again, this positive meaning must be determined epistemologically before it assumes a practical or political function. In other words, "Eurocentrism" belongs to a stage of critique that we have been engaged in for some time, on many different fronts, concerning the limits of what we can know (about ourselves), especially when we are solely dependent on the resources that have been provided by European traditions of thought and culture. However, in order to truly understand ourselves as belonging to this new movement of critical consciousness, we must again recall Foucault's caution concerning a too simplistic and much too authoritarian alternative. Recently, moreover, I have often heard it said that the permanent critique of ourselves in our autonomy – such as can be found in the critical traditions inaugurated for example by Foucault and Derrida – in the end gets us nowhere. Instead, what we really need (again) is a clear way out, a way to escape; we need to find something positive and affirmative on the other side, as in a completely different knowledge of ourselves.

It is not surprising, therefore, to see that this image of the escape from modernity, and the concomitant need to affirm something non-Eurocentric, has determined many of the theoretical positions over the last decade or so – even in a strategic sense of tactics devised to escape from the historical and philosophical legacy that has conditioned the very possibilities of the density of critical language we continue to employ to this day. As Derrida argued concerning a too simplistic understanding of the deconstructive method of displacement, it is not a matter of making what was formerly peripheral into a new center, in order to immediately discover the positive kernel of a new knowledge of ourselves, since this would simply be a form of logocentrism.

31

Rather, this historical process might be understood in a more Hegelian manner as representing only the first in a long series of dialectical reversals that must take place, given the fact that the new center will soon be shown to be limited in the knowledge it provides as well – which will lead to a second dialectical turning, and so on. Of course, such a critique has barely begun and should not be reserved only for those who are identified or who identify themselves as others from a certain perspective of the Subject that constitutes the central gaze of a colonizer. This would simply lead to a new form of dependence that would contradict the critical precept of the "creation of ourselves in our autonomy," that is, to a new form of essentialism (which is to say, new forms of humanism, or post-humanism). In the academic setting, of course, it is the ideology of what is called "strategic essentialism" that is really underscored by epistemological and institutional evaluations of prestige, by cultural elitism, even by the creation of new classes of intellectuals and thus new forms of intellectual snobbery. Thus, I do not buy the argument that a new form of essentialism – an essentialism of the oppressed, the formerly oppressed, or of the marginalized – will prove to be of greater value than the older forms of essentialism, since it is the very logic of essentialist discourse to affirm something positive at its core, something that is placed beyond negation, something that remains beyond reasoning or dispute, a hard kernel of reality whose truth is self-evident and must be acknowledged universally by everyone – or else! "Or else what?" To this question my interlocutor might reply, "nothing less than a complete and total negation of the Subject of the European Enlightenment itself," or at least of most of its historical representatives – a kind of "Exterminate all the brutes!" that is now directed against a new dark continent in thought.

If this trend represents one kind of severe reaction, or one strategy for escaping several centuries of error, another dominant trend that has occurred in contemporary theory is to jettison the position of the Subject altogether, as both the original and final cause of the History of Error and the condition of possibility for the form of error as such, creating instead a variety of "subjectless knowledges." If this solution appears rather extreme, it is nonetheless offered as our best hope for the future, since if the Subject is finally revealed as the source of all error, then erasing this perspective at the beginning of thought would amount to nothing less than removing all the barriers created especially by the Kantian critical philosophy, and especially concerning the finitude of our knowledge of the world, objects, all forms of life – but most importantly, concerning our knowledge of God. Consequently, one hallmark of current thinking shared by almost all the new methods and theories is the belief in a spontaneous and immediate access to those beings or entities that were formerly inhibited by the limitations of finitude in representational thought – that is, an access to things in themselves. This, however, is also coupled with an almost ecstatic exuberance concerning the possibilities of a thought that is finally emancipated from the severity of "Critique."

According to a small text published by Horkheimer (part of the later work with Adorno in *Philosophische Fragmente*), one of the first steps in recovering an original significance of *Aufklärung* would be for thinking to be emancipated from its fear of despair and pessimism. Most of all, as he writes, "to free Reason from the fear of being called nihilistic may be one of its steps to its recovery."[10] What Horkheimer is addressing in his own time concerns a peculiar development that could characterize our present moment as well: "there seems to be a mortgage on

33

any thinking, a self-imposed obligation to arrive at a cheerful conclusion."[11] Well, I hope you will not be offended if I say that this mortgage and this self-imposed obligation is very much a condition of our thinking today, that it could even be described in terms of a "blackmail," similar to the terms in which Foucault addressed the Enlightenment. Could this be a variation on Kant's famous maxim of theoretical-practical duty, "Dare to know (*sapere aude*), but above all, Obey!," which today might be recast as "Dare to know, but above all, be Positive!"? I might even call this the blackmail of cheeriness that characterizes much of what is called contemporary "critical theory." Of course, I am not using the word "positive" correctly, and "positivism" actually functions as a neologism in my own discourse. There is actually a kernel of the "positive-real" in discourse, which must be sharply distinguished from what Lacan called the kernel of the Real in both Symbolic and Imaginary constructions. The latter should always remain, in my view, like a bone cutting into the esophagus, something that you choke on, that suddenly catches you off guard, something that startles you. Sartre had already said, in *Being and Nothingness*, that the question has the same structure as destruction. Does this necessarily mean that all questions are nihilist at their core, or that the negativity of the question-form achieves the nothingness at the center of the Thing and exposes the thing itself to the nothingness that constitutes, in the manner of the virtual, its essence? In response, I would say this occurs only in those special cases where the act of questioning does not actually reveal something positive at the end of the process, but leaves the Thing empty and indefinite, that is, open to further determinations, leading all the way to a richness and complexity that most closely approximates our experience as such. In such cases, what is called "experience" comes at the end of the process, if it comes at all, and not at the beginning, and thus no longer resembles sense perception or common sense.

Returning to our contemporary maxim, or critical *ethos*, if we begin to think only under the condition that there is already a predetermined way out, would this not be a new dogmatic form of thought, to already have the exit plan before one even begins to think and to reason things out? Perhaps this is why many contemporary theories today seem to me more like articles of faith than lines of reasoning. More like a pleasant refrain in a favorite melody, something you can expect and even look forward to, something you can sing along to in moments of depression and fear. Is this obligation to arrive at cheerful conclusion – concerning the political, the coming community, religion ("without religion") and the multitude – is this actually shored up by the fear of despair, and a sign of "disillusionment" as Horkheimer suggested? What would be a thinking that might offer emancipation from this fear? Would this be nihilistic? It has always struck me as quite odd that those thinkers who are identified as nihilistic have often been the most affirmative. Nietzsche was a nihilist, if you remember, and Derrida and Foucault have also been identified as such – even worse, as "moral terrorists" – by some of their detractors. And yet, perhaps the nihilist procedure is the most critical one in the sense that at the most negative moment in the critique – we could call it its zenith – nothing is affirmed in place of the value, the idea, the notion that is torn down or destroyed, or at least, has been left suspended, and permanently in question.

In light of recent events, moreover, I wonder have we become nihilist enough? And yet, is it possible to "return to nihilism" without this in turn becoming a new exit strategy (that is, a new "return statement")? Would this be a return to a position of radical skepticism, cynicism, even Pyrrhonism? Perhaps, but why not? Are these not historical alternatives present in some version in every tradition? I have always wondered why these are immediately determined as "bad" choices among all the alternatives we have to choose from today. No doubt, this question has emerged from recent experiences that are both intensely personal and also "world-historical." Thus I have come to this point in understanding my own critical *ethos*, and become ready to make the following experiment in the investigation of "our contemporary reality." What would it mean, I ask myself, if one were to actually risk *believing in nothing* – neither in revolution nor emancipation, nor in poetry or love, nor in religion or the myth of friendship (i.e., politics). Certainly not in "Humanity!" (As the lawyer once exclaimed to Bartleby, "Oh Humanity!")

And yet, this must be understood strictly as an experiment conducted on myself, in the manner Foucault first defined in the article I have been addressing, as strictly a "historico-practical test of the limits that we may go beyond, and thus as a work that is carried out by ourselves upon ourselves as free beings."[12] Thus, to think without a predetermined "exit-strategy" or "self-imposed mortgage on our own thinking" is to appeal to an original image of reason defined by Kant as "pure reason" (*reinen Vernunf*), which must also include the possibilities of "reasoning for the sake of reasoning" and even "arguing for the sake of arguing" (*räsonieren*), both of which have been determined historically by the pejorative term "rationalism" (but only when the idea of reason assumes a positivist value and, thus, is neither completely "pure" nor strictly "free" to think anything it wants, and for no other reason than reason itself). Am I calling for a "return to rationalism" then? Or a position of radical *skepsis*, a suspension of belief? Maybe so, and why not? Especially given the alternatives we currently have available to us. I have recently come to the conclusion that, at least, we should dare again to know the limitations of our belief in this world.

Notes

A previous version of this statement appeared as "*Sapere Aude?*," *Symploke* 14:1–2 (2007), pp. 35–42.

1 Talking Heads, *Stop Making Sense*, Palm Pictures, 1984.
2 Green, "Modern Culture Comes of Age: Hamann versus Kant on the Root Metaphor of the Enlightenment," p. 292.
3 Ibid.
4 Godzich, "Caution! Reader at Work!," in De Man, *Blindness and Insight*, p. xv.
5 Barthes, *Mythologies*, pp. 151–2.
6 Horkheimer, "Reason Against Itself: Some Remarks on Enlightenment," p. 336.
7 Foucault, "What is Enlightenment?," p. 43.
8 Ibid., p. 43.
9 Ibid., p. 47.
10 Horkheimer, "Reason Against Itself: Some Remarks on Enlightenment," p. 336.
11 Ibid.
12 Foucault, "What is Enlightenment?," p. 47.

2

"What's Love Got to do With it?"

It has been said that we are living in an age of post-secularism, or the "return of religion." The signs of this return are everywhere, and not only in the Islamic world, but in the former West as well – the return of fundamentalisms, ethnocentrisms, "integrisms" of culture and race, religious wars, even a war to end all positive religions. Sometimes, these signs are missiles, or bodies that fall helplessly from the sky like leaves. Sometimes they are earthquakes or tsunamis, announcing the judgment of God. But there is also another class of signs, no less prophetic, that announce the moment when God finally succumbs to something like a peaceful (albeit not natural) death, at the very moment when the word "religion" itself loosens its death grip on life, and turns about into a new openness, a new horizon, a new hope for religion without "religion." It is around these two classes of signs, even these two names of God, these two senses that can be accorded to the phrase the "return of religion" (with or without "religion"), that I wish to investigate the recent theological writings of John D. Caputo.

Before doing so, however, I want to recall an episode from the life of the late-contemporary American poet James Wright. In his poetry, Wright often reflected upon a contradictory social characteristic of the human animal whose exceptional nature lies in its boundless capacity for love, but also in the excessiveness of its demand for love from others. Wright once addressed this directly in a letter he wrote to the poet and novelist Leslie Silko a year before his death.[1] In it he responds to a passage from Silko's previous letter where she talks about the death of a pet rooster which, she confesses, the family had loved in a "strange sort of way." I will quote this earlier passage from Silko's letter, since it is important in understanding the brooding intensity of Wright's response, an intensity that is important for the context of this discussion.

> He was a mean and dirty bird but we loved him in a strange sort of way. Our friends who had been pursued or jumped by this rooster find it difficult to appreciate our loss. I guess I am still surprised by the feeling I had for him – to realize that without wanting to, without any reason to, he had been dear to us. We are told that we should only love the good and the beautiful, and these are defined for us so narrowly. Monday I will be 31. Maybe it has taken me this long to discover that we are liable to love anything – like characters in old Greek stories who set eyes on an oak tree or a bucket and fall in love hopelessly, there are no limits to our love.[2]

In his reply written twelve days later from Verona, Italy, Wright responds with the following passage:

> What you wrote about the improbability of loving this fierce little creature struck me very deep, because your words are so close to a passage from Spinoza's Ethics. The passage has given me some pain, but finally it is heartening and bracing, because it is, in my view, the clearest statement of the plain truth that I know. Spinoza says that the human being is a miraculous creature, and his miracle consists in his capacity for love. He

39

can love anything, from an atom all the way to God. But it is just here, says Spinoza that a tragic difficulty arises. For man must realize that his capacity for love gives him no right in demanding that anyone love him in return. Not anyone. Not even God. I have found that a hard thing to face, but there is something in it that goes beyond pain.[3]

What must have terrified Wright and motivated him to respond with such seriousness to Silko's anecdote about the death of the pet rooster was probably her last remark: "There are no limits to our love." We could modify this phrase in order to read it the way Wright most likely understood it: *There are no limits to our unconscious and often insane demand for love from others.*

In modern urban societies, in particular, the different expressions of this demand are linked to the social production of a "non-knowledge" that daily threatens individual identity on all sides and that can be inferred from the most common and everyday appearances of anonymity, forgetting, enmity, denial, oppression, and estrangement (or alienation). These are the implicate forms of an unconscious order that conditions the most quotidian relationships, marking a social present for the individual whose identity is bordered on each side by a threat of annihilation. "You are for Us," a certain group, class, or social cell might say, "or you don't exist – you are nothing for Us and, consequently, no-one." Silently and implicitly, this Either/Or constitutes what I would call the social present tense and represents a dominant factor of socialization, one which can be found at the heart of every extended family, every professional organization, every workplace or cocktail party, every school or university, organized religion, ethnic or political community. The very existence of the modern individual, an existence which can only be established from the standpoint of the recognition by an

"Other," is shaped by the continuous force of annihilation which decides the question "to be, or not to be" in the most decisive manner. At its extreme points, however, either symptomatically or perhaps essentially, this threat must be brought into contact with the more extreme collective expressions of social hatred (or enmity), historical repression, and even with a certain genocidal desire that lies at the basis of historical societies. Ironically, we have discovered that it is sometimes this same principle of personal identity and communal belonging that also accounts for the strange and paradoxical logic that makes the hatred of strangers and the persecution of certain "others" with the threat of extinction and non-identity a necessary consequence.

In *Civilization and its Discontents*, Freud described how the antithetical attributes of love and hatred determine the essential "civilizing" character of modern societies generally and of modern Christian societies in particular. The excessive demand that characterizes love is what conditions and inflames the excessive cruelty that underscores hatred; therefore, we can understand the demand that founds and conditions both notions as a kind of "discontent" that afflicts Christian civilization. This is because in the current arrangement of social interest, the profound intensity of love can only be defined against an equally profound intensity of hatred, just as a "blessing" only appears against the profile of a "curse." A society whose fundamental organizing principle and ethical injunction to "bind together" – Come! – is founded upon the absolute right to demand love from everyone (and equally the right to hate, to curse, and to annihilate all those who do not comply with this demand) is also a society whose notions of social existence, identity, recognition, prestige (or *fama*) are predicated on the threats of anonymity and personal extinction, as well as the annihilation and social forgetting of what is "proper" to the name: the being-in-common it signifies for the one who bears it as a distinct "property." We can find examples of these notions at every level, in every community, cultural institution, and social enclave of our current society. It would be fair to infer from these examples, if we took the time to collate them, the presence of an organizing principle, which governs the current arrangement of social interest that Freud called "the death drive" (*Todestrieb*). In view of this principle, we might take note of Freud's somewhat uncharacteristic emotional outcry in *Civilization and its Discontents* made in response to the Christian commandment "Love thy neighbor as thyself": Why should we do this? Freud asked.[4] What good is it to us? Above all, how can we do such a thing? How can it possibly be done?

At the origin of Christianity we find the purest expression of the intense ambivalence that shapes and conditions the duality in the concept of love. The symbol of this ambivalence is a tree on which a man is strung up. In the different poetic representations of this symbol, there are sometimes two trees and two men depicted. The tree upon which Christ was hung won him universal love, while the tree upon which Judas hung won him universal enmity. If the passion of Christ marks the transubstantiation of death, the curse of life, into the highest blessing, then the passion of Judas marks the transubstantiation of its blessing, birth, into the strongest curse. The two trees of Judas Iscariot and Jesus Christ mark the purest moral expression of the ambivalence that shapes human judgment. The hatred that is bestowed upon the criminal marks the recognition, on the part of community, of a form of love that remains "outside" incorporation (a form of loss, a denial or negation of the social demand); it is opposed to the demand for love from an individual whose gift of death marks a fundamental event of the community's own self-constitution which, in Hegelian language, marks the conversion of the individual's "in-itself" into the "for-us." Ultimately, I think this bipolar or "two-tree theory" is a subterfuge and a compromise formation with regard to the fairly commonplace morality that asserted itself in the subsequent renderings of the meaning of this symbol. The subterfuge was placed there to conceal the fact that there is only one tree, representing the family of the human being, and on this tree hangs a son who is loved by his father and mourned by his mother, and at the same time, a stranger and a criminal who is hated and despised, a murderer who is cast out and murdered by his society, despised by his father who turns his face away from him, forgotten by his mother, a man with no qualities (other than the name of criminal that is assigned to him by a society of strangers) who is condemned to die alone. Against the tradition that has misinterpreted this symbol, I would say that there is only one man, who is both loved and hated in a single act. I often think that the profundity of Christianity, in its original sense, was to divinize this intense and intensely contradictory spirit of ambivalence that is the paradox of human community. How can the same man be both a criminal and a God? A son loved by his father and mourned by his mother and, at the same time, a stranger who is cast out and whose body is turned into carrion left for the birds to devour. As you can see, I would see this dilemma as the same as that which motivated Sophocles to dramatize this very same question even earlier in *Antigone* (441 B.C.E.). But there again, we have two men or two brothers, one who is a hero (or God) and one who is hated (a criminal); it is only Antigone who sees them as one man, and she in turn, contradicts the moral sentiment of the city and must kill herself in the end to embody this contradiction as a sign that is sent so that future communities may decipher it, but remains to a large degree indecipherable, all the way up to the present day. That is, she cannot bear the contradiction and sees it as proof of the impossibility of love – and so she denies herself the possibility of love that was assigned to her gender and social position (in the "either/or" character of being a mother or a bride) and, instead, throws herself into the void. I would argue that it is from this same void that Christianity emerged 500 years later in the Roman World.

So again, like Antigone, I take it that the original dilemma posed in the Christian myth was to admit that these two men were, in fact, the same man and that subsequently a commonplace morality was invented to separate them out again, to justify why one man is loved and the other hated and despised. This is a simple moral notion that evacuates the concept of love in this religion and turns it once again into a justification for every social division, for war, and, ultimately, for genocide. The concept of love that we have inherited from this tradition is guilty of any number of these historically, and in this regard its morality is no different than that of other religions founded on a deep sense of familialism and ethnocentrisms. Thus, this notion of love is predicated upon a notion of hatred and enmity, and can easily be used to divide those I love and who are close to me and my neighbors from those others and strangers who I am justified in hating – especially when they are "evil." On the other hand, in the original symbol, we have a glimpse of another kind of love, one that is infinitely divided within itself, contradictory, admitting in its heart a very profound sense of ambivalence. This is the love of a father for his son, who, precisely because he loves him, kills him (or lets him be killed).

All this functions as a prefatory remark to explain the reaction I had when I recently read Caputo's *On Religion* (without religion), wherein I found a lot of talk about love, but very little discussion of the kind of love we have inherited from this tradition, the kind that is bordered by hatred and social demand, and, at its furthest border, by a threat of annihilation. In fact, by technically employing what is called a phenomenological reduction (*epokē*), Caputo "brackets" (or in Heidegger's usage, particularly in the *Seinsfrage*, "crosses out or through [*durchstreichen*]," or in Derrida's phrasing of this same technique, "places under erasure [*sous rature*]") both "Love" and "God" in the phrase "the Love of God." The lines crossed through these words are invisible, but they are nevertheless there, and this gesture is made in order to indicate that when we read these words or proper names we should not immediately understand them in their ontic, historical, significance, "because the Love of God cannot be defined – or contained – by religion. The Love of God is too important to leave to the religions or the theologians." Thus, by means of this bracketing operation of its ontico-ontological senses, "the name of God, and the Love of God, can stay clear of all the complications of human 'religion.'" (Note that in this last instance, the word religion is placed in quotation marks.[5])

Well, this is a neat trick, and it is certainly one way to talk about Religion (without "religion") whilst avoiding "religion." But I wonder if it could be that simple, that is, if the reduction risks not complicating things enough, risks losing the name altogether? As Heidegger cautioned concerning this technique when he employed it on the word "Being," it is inherently risky and should only be employed with the greatest of care (*Sorge*) and with the most rigorous sense of obligation to the name's essence, since in detaching the sense of the name from its significance, which is multiple, one risks sending it off into nothingness and unthinkability, into "non-sense." So this will be my question today: whether the use of this technique opens the name to a more essential repetition of its meaning or whether it exposes the name to a loss of meaning (to a "weak" or a "non-essential repetition") and should therefore be judged a methodological failure. And I will pose this question particularly as it concerns the reduction or bracketing of two words in Caputo's text: "Love" and "the Good." My thesis will be that in his representations of Love, what Caputo crosses-through or cancels out is precisely the character of demand that functions as its support and, in a certain sense, its guarantee: an obligation "to come together." It is only on the basis of this social demand that any sense of ethical obligation can be said to persist, in a "weak" sense, even in the linguistic and performative sense as what binds the subject to a certain promise, as what allows one to speak of love with any certainty that it will be present from one moment to the next.

Of course, there is a certain sense of demand or obligation in the background of Caputo's representation, and it functions as a motivation for the ethical injunctions to feed the poor and hungry, clothe and house the homeless, to welcome the stranger and the refugee, to love justice. But then, these are the same kind of garden variety injunctions that one might hear in Sunday school, which means that they are said to make one feel good in saying them, because, from a Lyotardian perspective, they do not even function as prescriptive phrases, as phrases of obligation. Let us take some examples. In *On Religion*, Caputo writes: "Lovers are people who exceed their duty, who look around for ways to do more than is required of them."[6] Well, I have to say that this sounds like the wisdom of someone who says "if you love your job, then you should do more than is required of you." This is the universal maxim of a shop-boss or a foreman. What is missing is precisely the character of demand, and of a certain threat at its core: If you want to keep your job, then you better show your love by always doing more than is asked of you. The one who does not love their job in this manner sooner or later gets fired. Likewise, the statement: "If you love your children, what would you not do for them?" Well, I have to say, in response, there are a lot of things I could think of, and not just unethical things like bludgeoning one of their playmates for giving your child a bump on the head (although what parent hasn't enjoyed the fantasy of beating into a pulp the insolent little kid down the block who has learned the human art of cruelty a little too well). There's a lot of things I wouldn't do for my children, and then there are things I have done, but that I certainly didn't want to do for them, but was constrained by a certain notion of "the Good." Children are extremely shrewd in this regard and sooner or later every parent is subjected to the unconditional demand: "If you love me, then you will do anything for me." It is precisely at these crucial ethical moments that a parent has to hold her position, as the one who phrases the demand into a certain theoretical maxim of duty, one which should never be applied to concrete relationships. However, if the parent does acquiesce, submitting herself to the child's universal demand for the proof of love, then both will encounter the limit of love, that is to say its impossibility.

In his earlier work *Against Ethics*, in a discussion of the love for "the Good," Caputo admits at one point: "I have a maximally weak and non-constraining notion of the Good, one which reminds me of one of the most beautiful maxims of the medieval masters: *dilige, et vis quod fac*: Love, and do what you will."[7] When I read this, I was struck by an uncanny resemblance to a general sentiment I found in *On Religion*, and the same could be said for Caputo's notion of Love as "a maximally weak and non-constraining notion."[8] In turn, I wondered if Caputo was mixing up the two notions, mixing up or con-fusing Love and the Good. What does one love in the Good, or rather, what is the Good in Love, or even, is it always Good to Love? It is at this point I might recall one of the most beautiful maxims by another contemporary master – "What's love got to do with it?"[9]

First of all, what has love got to do with the Good, properly speaking? Technically, the Good is often posed as an object of Love. The Good is the love-object *sine qua non*. But to Love is itself Good, or the Good in itself. One loves to be in Love with the Good. Of course, in resolving this problem of attribution, I would prefer to turn to psychoanalysis, which I think is a lot more helpful than Aquinas or Augustine in this regard, even at the risk of losing Caputo, whose "maximally weak and non-constraining notions" are not very helpful either, I must confess. As Saint Thomas argued, in loving God, we love the Good in ourselves – only the English language affords us the accidental "o" to form the difference between God and the Good. This is fortuitous, since this little "o" stands for an object that I love that stands in place of God in the above equation. In this object, we invest a lot. In this moment, we love what is best in ourselves, we share the same object as what God loves as well. Of course, here there is a contradiction, because it is well known that two people cannot love the same thing, especially when the thing in question is a person, and so there is a potential conflict that must be shifted elsewhere. For Lacan, this conflict is shifted to the sexual relation. Let me clarify: two people cannot love in themselves in the same object, which is the ego, which is why this object is mediated by the field of language, which is to say

48

that it is always found to be divided up unequally; therefore, Lacan's simple maxim is "I love in you something more than you." This is a simple explanation, by the way, of why the sexual relation does not work.

Secondly, from the perspective of the psychoanalytic theory of Love, as opposed to the Thomist physical theory, one can certainly say that the Good is the source of Love, but at the same time, it is also that strange quasi-object that lands on certain real objects and causes them to become both interesting and attractive. The Good is the source (in the sense of *Quelle*), that is to say, it is also the aim of the drive (*Trieb*). In the original division of the Subject, at the moment that the ego is constituted as separated from the world of objects, Lacan says that something flies off, escapes, which causes the ego to turn its attention to the world in search of it. He called it the myth of the "lamella."[10] This something could be said to be a little bit of the Good that the ego has lost in foregoing its primary narcissism. But this also implies that this little piece of eternity, this lamella, this primary narcissism, has escaped and is suddenly out there in the world somewhere, and the ego is magically converted into a knight who is constantly on a quest to find it. It is for this reason that the notion of the Good often returns as a source of anxiety, as a reminder of this loss and original division, or why an object that is suddenly found (or re-found) to locate the missing Good is always filled at the same time with ambivalence, or can suddenly turn its face away and repeat that trauma of original separation. This is what gives the Good its magical vanishing character – now you see it now you don't – and it is often the case that the minute the ego stumbles onto something good, it jumps at the chance to possess it or to swallow it down in one bite, at the risk, of course, of destroying the object that was its momentary support.

All of this is fairly rudimentary and mundane. From a more Freudian perspective, it is only the function of immemorial and unconscious guilt that intervenes to save the object, an immemorial mourning over the murder of the Good, that commands or exhorts the ego to try to find another way to "enjoy" the object than through incorporation or destruction. Therefore, on the one hand, the Good becomes identified with a particular class of objects that appear indestructible, or which appear outside the ego's power to ingest and incorporate them, and the Good is indeed preserved according to this technique as the endless reservoir of the ego's own self-love. On the other hand, the Good is endowed with a character of indestructibility like those victims described by de Sade whose bodies become more glorious the more they are made filthy and defiled, which, according to psychoanalysis, is transferred onto the sexual relation. Consequently, the more you defile yourself, according to the command of the ego, the more you prove your Love.

In my view, this is where we have to return to Spinoza for some hint of an answer, in some ways following Wright's observation concerning our unconscious and insane demand for the love of another. In the *Ethics*, Spinoza offers something of an explanation of how Loving the Good can take on either a sadistic or a masochistic character. By sadistic, I mean an action of hatred addressed toward another person, that is, toward the very "well-being" of the other person, which is the object of annihilation in sadism; by masochistic, I understand this hatred being directed toward an object, and to the body itself bound up with pleasure and pain as the primary object in masochism. Spinoza writes: "If a man has begun to hate a beloved thing, so that his love of it is altogether destroyed, he will for this reason hate it more than he would have done had he never loved it, and his hatred will be greater in proportion to his previous love."[11] As Spinoza explains, because love is joy "which a man endeavors to preserve as much as possible" – by maintaining the beloved object's presence, and by affecting it with his joy as much as possible (that is, by loving it) – when love turns to hatred, these actions must be constrained by an incredible effort or will. According to this description, joy is not simply converted into sadness but rather into hatred, which reverses the previous relation to the beloved object, as Spinoza says, in a proportion greater than the original love: the object must be made to be absent, by an act of will on the part of the lover (that is, the beloved cannot simply withdraw of his or her own will, or merely be absent, but must be sent off into nothingness). Secondly, the previous affection of joy must be replaced by a greater affection of sadness inflicted on the beloved (that is, in memory, the beloved is submitted to all sorts of phantasies and tortures that extract from the beloved a greater degree of enjoyment than even love had provided). Of course, anyone who has been involved in a divorce or break-up would never confess to all the ways in which the beloved is violated by the most grotesque of means, usually in highly symbolic acts directed against the beloved's own sense of "well-being."

Here, I recall the story of a man who, after his offer of engagement was interrupted by the news of a sexual affair, sent his token of love, a ring, to his former beloved in a box of his own feces. In some ways this perfectly illustrates the actions that Spinoza describes above – not only because it is a highly symbolic act on many different levels, and concerns the symbolism of the ring in particular (which is infused with a kind of joy that is purported to be unparalleled and even transcends the joy of the sexual act), but because this act is pure and completely useless from a utilitarian point of view – as an expenditure or sacrifice.

51

After all, he could have simply returned the ring and got his $10,000 dollars back and put it down instead on a new luxury item or some other object that would have afforded him some pleasure in compensation for his loss. Instead, he sacrificed the possibility of such an exchange, since the money itself was now defiled and had lost its function as capital; in a highly symbolic gesture attesting to this fact, he fashioned a signifier that vividly illustrated his affect and reduced the image of the beloved to a little pile of his own excrement bearing the token and the promise of his eternal hatred. Of course, at the end of this little love story, the beloved, upon receiving this token, immediately washed it off in the kitchen sink and took it to the jeweler, after which she sent a note to the man saying "Thank you very much for the new car. It is what I have always wanted." Her response was extremely significant and a brilliant deconstruction of the commodity character of sexual exchange, since for her the greatest pain she could possibly imagine inflicting was to demonstrate that, for her, his sexual love was easily exchangeable (or was equivalent to her pleasure from commodities) and that she could associate his absence with the possibility of pleasure derived from other objects. Thus, the man's letter was returned to him, in a certain sense, unopened (or opened inside-out, as Lacan would say, his own message communicated back to him in reverse form), since it clearly did not have the affect he intended it to have, but quite the opposite. Rather, for him, it had the affect of binding her gesture to a certain murder of the Good, which Spinoza defines as "anything that satisfies longing, whatever it may be" (Proposition 39, note), including, I might add here, the longing associated with annihilating the possibility of the joy for the beloved, of damaging her feeling of "well-being," and replacing it with an eternal sadness, which functioned as his own highest Good and the object of longing on this occasion. (If anyone would argue that the Good cannot be an object of hatred, I would refer them again to Spinoza, since this is how I understand the statement "anything that satisfies longing, whatever it may be.") In the end, as you might have anticipated, upon receiving the note the man returned to his beloved's house, knocked her unconscious, and then handcuffed her to the steering wheel of her new car, turning the engine on and closing the garage door. One could only imagine the satisfaction that this act brought him, particularly when he phantasized about the neighbors and the police finding her bloated and asphyxiated body several days later, and the sense of stupor at the manner of the murder, the meaning of which only he could enjoy, given the irony that he had simply revised his original message by substituting the earlier metaphors for their original signifieds, since she was in fact wearing the ring after all and her body was now the equivalent of his earlier symbolic representative.

As Lacan writes in the seminar *Encore*, in a little section dedicated to the mysteries of Love, "for Empedocles, God was the most ignorant of all beings because he had no knowledge of hatred. Later, Christians transformed this into torrents of love. Unfortunately, it doesn't work because to be without knowledge of hatred, is also to be without knowledge of love. If God does not know hatred, it is clear for Empedocles that he knows less than mortals."[12] Recalling Spinoza's proposition, it is clear that hatred is borne of love, and moreover, has greater intensity. If I have emphasized the symbolic character so much, it is to show the diversity of the Good that hatred can create. Hatred can fashion the Good "out of anything whatsoever," whereas I would argue that the capacity for imagining the Good as the ultimate object of Love appears somewhat impoverished – or "weak" – by comparison, particularly the abstract Good that emerges to represent the Love of God as a common notion. And yet, there may be some benefit in imagining a notion of the Good as a "weak and nonconstraining notion," after all, and perhaps the Love of God should be weak and nonconstraining in order to prevent hatred from entering into the world from the same source. Hatred can only be borne out of Love, the more intense hatred would be borne from "the torrents of love" introduced by Christianity; likewise, according to Lacan, this weak and nonconstraining notion of Love could only be Christian. Perhaps it would be better not to Love at all – not a God, not even an atom – certainly it might be better for the other upon whom we bestow our own "torrents of love," if only to guarantee the other's love in return with an implacable demand and the threat of hatred and annihilation should the other leave. But here again, to recall Wright's earlier comment, the tragic difficulty arises. For as long as the opposite of love is hatred, and not knowledge, then this tragic "Either/Or" may be the only possibility for the other to exist as an object worthy of our Love in the first place.

So again, I return to my refrain, what's love got to do with it? This time, however, I will ask what has love got to do with knowledge? This is because it is precisely when I am in love that I am not in knowledge. I could try and say my love in words, but words fail, and inevitably I begin talking non-sense. And perhaps this is precisely the point, that there is something unconscious that must be present for one to feel in love, something of a "*je ne sais quoi*," and it is in this non-knowledge that one finds a certain enjoyment, a little piece of the lamella that was previously lost. It is in the direct relation between the experience of non-knowledge and the feeling of love that

Christianity has played a fundamental role, which was later on transformed by bourgeois social relations, since whom I choose to love cannot be determined strictly by symbolic factors – by class, kinship relations, race or ethnicity – even though at bottom all these factors of the Symbolic determine the object of my choice in a manner that analysis might someday clarify with a computer-generated equation resembling differential calculus. In place of hopelessly trawling through the world, haunted by contingency and chance, in search of our beloved object, we might simply visit a data bank to discover who our perfect object-choice is, and even clarify the enigma of our own sexuality for an additional fee (queer, straight, gay, trans); even better, perhaps this will be done in the same way that we are now issued social security cards. This seems very unlikely, however, since even if such knowledge was available we would probably want to know nothing of it, and would rather remain blissfully ignorant, wanting to "enjoy" our unconscious and thus to willfully retain our passivity in relation to the sudden "torrents of love." Perhaps this is a different way of understanding the maxim "Love, and do what you will." *Being in Love, one wills to go unconscious and to become as stupid as God in such matters.* But God's non-knowledge of hatred cannot be passed off as simple ignorance, since it entails a stronger sense of unconscious knowledge closer to denial or disavowal. In the being of God we deny our own knowledge of the hatred that serves as the support for our Love, which seems like erecting a God whose "goodness" can only serve to reinforce this denial: A weak God, therefore, is simply more stupid and thus more blissful than Man about the reality of the Unconscious. And yet, the reason this notion of Love doesn't work for Man is because, without a little hatred mixed in, love loses its salt, if we understand by hatred the passions of jealously, possession, fear, etc. – in other words, the degree of intensity that characterizes these emotions, which form the reverse proof of the intensity associated with "the torrents of love."

What is interesting in this statement is that Christians were the first to transform God's non-knowledge of hatred into torrents of love. Lacan's proof was the mystics themselves, whose torrents of love for God, in a devotion that often surpasses a simple phallic enjoyment of well-being, comes off looking a lot like, well, acts of self-hatred directed against their own bodies which are now seen as obstacles to God's love. In short, the mystics simply reintroduced the sexual relation into their under-standing of the love of God. But if to love the best in oneself is to enjoy God's own perfect love, then the mystics' manner of loving God "in a strange sort of way" is something that can't really be accounted for by Aquinas' physical theory of Love. Earlier on, the French philosopher and writer Georges Bataille explored the mystical relation to Love, arguing that "more than any believer, Christian mystics crucify Jesus." The mystic's love requires a God to risk himself, to shriek out in despair on the cross." Thus, the basic crime associated with the saints is erotic, related to "the transports and tortured fevers that produce burning love in the monasteries and the convents."[13] In one sense, the mystical suffering acts out the inherent contradiction in Christianity that I noted earlier – that God so loved the world that he tortured and murdered his beloved object. The mystic shares with God in this tragic action, crucifying the image of Jesus in her own flesh in order to experience the ecstatic nature of God's exorbitant loss in a frenzy of self-immolation, in order finally to attain a point that is "beyond pleasure and pain," which Bataille identifies as the "summit of desire." Recalling Spinoza's description of the conversion of the beloved object from love to hatred, the mystic exerts an incredible will to cause this object to become absent, and through this constraining action (the fantasy of crucifying her beloved object again and again) enacts an intensity that is greater in proportion to the original feeling of love that had existed for Jesus before, a love now tinged with eroticism and the guilt associated with sharing responsibility for God's insane and senseless act.

Although this intensity is defined by Spinoza as hatred, we need not imagine that there is only one emotional state that is contrary to love; the intensity associated with vice also occupies a pole that is opposite to love, only in a different direction. In fact, in a parallel proposition to the one I earlier cited where Spinoza argues that hatred is stronger in intensity than the love of the object it has supplanted, he admits that love can surpass hatred in intensity only on those occasions when the object of love was previously hated (given that the physical state of hatred remains present as a condition and is only acted upon and converted by a constraining act of will on the part of the subject, just as the physical relation of love remains latent in the subsequent act of hating the beloved). In a very revealing note to this proposition, Spinoza raises the possibility of this desire in a manner that perfectly describes the mystical conversion of sorrow into joy, but then dismisses it as absurd. He remains, in this regard, too much the rationalist. I will quote this note in full:

> Notwithstanding the truth of this passage, no one will try and hate a thing or will wish to be affected with sorrow in order that he may rejoice the more, that is to say, no one will desire to inflict loss on himself in the hope of recovering the loss, or become ill in the hope of getting well, in as much as everyone will always try and preserve his being and remove sorrow from

himself as much as possible. Moreover, if it can be imagined that it would be possible for us to desire to hate a person in order that we may love him afterwards the more, we must always desire to continue the hatred. For the love will be the greater as the hatred has been greater, and therefore we shall always desire that the hatred be more and more increased. Upon the same principle we shall desire that our sickness may continue and even increase in order that we may afterwards enjoy the greater pleasure when we get well, and therefore shall always desire sickness, which is absurd. (Proposition 44, scholia)[14]

But then, this seems like a perfect explanation for the mystical equation, when the previous hatred of the flesh in normal Christian morality becomes the support for the transformation of this object as expressing a new intensity of love by the constraining action that the mystic performs on her own body in order to experience "a summit of desire" that was previously unattainable, an orgasm not only of the flesh but of the soul (or mind) as well.[15] In a very interesting passage, Bataille comments on the eschewing of this more primitive and orgiastic "summit of desire," and even its criminalization as a form of vice by modern Christian civilization. Nevertheless, it continues to persist in two special areas of social life: first, in the private sphere of the modern bourgeois individual pertaining especially to the experience of "Romantic Love" (this becomes Lacan's special area of investigation, to which I shall return below); and, secondly, in discursive representations whereby the destruction of the flesh effected in real drunken orgies and sacrifices takes on an abstract and highly symbolic form of lyrical expression and meditational and confessional subjects dedicated to the mysteries of Love. Concerning this second development, Bataille writes in *On Nietzsche*:

> Clearly ... whether we are dealing with yogis, Buddhists, or Christian monks, there is no reality to [the utter ruin and expenditure that the mystic desires] ..., to such perfections associated with desire. With them, crime or the annihilation of existence is a representation. Their general compromise with regard to morality can easily be shown. Real license was rejected from the arena of the possible as being fraught with unpleasant consequences: orgies or sacrifices, for instance. But since there remains the desire for a summit with which these acts are connected, and since beings are still under the necessity of "communicating" with their beyond, symbols (or fictions) have replaced reality. The sacrifice of the mass as representing the reality of the death of Jesus is simply a symbol of the infinite renewal of the church. Meditational subjects have take the place of real orgies, drunkenness, and flesh and blood – the latter becoming objects of disapproval. In this way there still remained a summit connected with desire, while the various violations of existence that were connected with that summit no longer were compromising, since now they had become mental representations.[16]

At the same time, perhaps there is a remainder of Lacan's "torrents of love" (or Bataille's "desire for the summit") which can actually be found at the bottom of the phrase "prayers and tears" such as this phrase functions as a performative formula in Caputo's work. But, we might ask, are these real prayers, or real tears, or rather just "mental representations"? After all, at the risk of provocation, one wonders what is at stake in Caputo's gesture of making such a scene as crying in public, of being a big cry-baby, even though the place where he chooses to make such a scene is highly discursive, rationalized and logically constructed, and is bound to the necessity of "communicating" something by means of these purely symbolic wails and these fictional tears. Nevertheless, following Bataille's argument, the desire for the summit remains, but has been given an abstract and meditational subject, which is "the Love of God." As Caputo exclaims, "I take my stand with love, and with God, and I am driven by a passion for God" ("torrents of love"?).[17]

In the final section of *Prayers and Tears*, under the proposition "I do not know what I Love when I Love my God," we find again, precisely, this "non-knowledge" characterized as "a dark and secret passion":

> To be in the secret does not mean you know anything. But not to know anything, *sans voir, sans avoir, sans savoir*, does not means to drift despondently from day to day, in a cloud of unknowing and uncaring, but to dream – "hoping, sighing, dreaming" – of something unforeseeable, unpossessable, undreamt of, unknowable, of which the eye has not seen or the ear heard. To dream, perchance, to desire and to love. And what is that dream, desire, and love if not the love of God? If not the desire for God ("God as the other name for desire")? What is this passion for the impossible if not this passion for God, for "my God," even if one were rightly to pass for an atheist? When something unforeseeable and unknowable, unpossessable and impossible drives us mad, when the *tout autre* becomes the goal, without goal, the object without object, of a dream and desire that renounces its own momentum of appropriation, when the impossible is the object of our love and passion, is that what we mean by "my God"? Is that not the name of God? Is that not a name that we would bend every effort to save, with or without religion?[18]

I must confess, in response to this final question, there is something in all these statements that passes all understanding, something of a love that seeks to go unconscious, "to dream, perchance, to desire," which is perhaps a different way of understanding the statement, "to go with God." Rather than taking the time that a deconstruction of this passage might involve – there is not enough time – I will simply come back to underline this character of "non-knowledge" that pertains to the Love of God that is particularly Christian. Again, this "non-knowledge" cannot be defined as simply ignorance or unconsciousness, because it is also the source of an intensity, the source of a passion. To return to Spinoza, passions only characterize the relation between inadequate ideas and their objects, since adequate ideas express an active relation to their objects that Spinoza identifies with the act of thinking itself. Therefore, what constitutes a passion is "the unthought," which can be formulated as that place or that occasion where the Subject does not think to think. And it is important to note that Spinoza admits that the Christian love of God expresses an inadequate idea concerning the other objects that he contains within him (first of all, it expresses an inadequate idea pertaining to the object of his own body, which Spinoza spends a great deal of time discussing in his discussion of the prophetic representation of God's body in the *Theological-Political Treatise*).[19] Earlier we have characterized "hatred" as an inadequate idea that is contained in the notion of the Christian God, an idea that is also a source of passion that Spinoza attempts to clarify in the *Ethics*. However, from a psychoanalytic point of view, this particular form of non-knowledge and this source of passion cannot but be placed in relation to an object that is situated for the human being in the field of sexuality, in relation to which the subject first emerges qua Subject, that is, is subjected to the signifier that will be the source of passion and non-knowledge, but of love and hatred as well. This is a fundamental perspective that could be defined as the materialist point of view its knowledge of this object attempts to clarify, even in making of it an adequate idea.

That is to say, it is not a theology, which means that neither Freud nor the later Lacan went about celebrating this non-knowledge and turning it into an object of poetry, or ritual sacrifice, but were rather concerned with the future of this object, in as much as it remains stubbornly stuck in the Real, expressed in the form of an inadequate idea, an idea that holds the human being completely captivated (e.g., as a "slave to love," like a "slave to Christ"). Of course, in response to this situation the character of Freud's pessimism is well known, a trait that is only highlighted in Lacanian hysteria over what he called "the dark Christian God of sacrifice" that rules over this world and possibly the next one as well. My only concern is that we are still not skeptical enough about this "dark God of sacrifice," and, moreover, that it is only in approaching a knowledge of hatred that we might someday understand the function of love. As Lacan seems to be implying, it simply doesn't work the other way around – that in seeking a knowledge of love we come to understand hatred. And perhaps this is the basis for understanding the very different approaches toward knowledge between a psychoanalytic and a theological point of view, if only because from the perspective of psychoanalytic knowledge, "God is also the name of desire," but then, this is not a cause for celebration, for weeping and dancing, but for "prayers and tears" of a very different kind. It is a cause for incredible pain and sorrow, because as Levinas first observed, "the Ego is Love-sick."

If I have spent a great deal of time discussing the psycho-analytic approach to the notions of "Love" and "the Good" it is, in part, to call attention to a place in Caputo's own text where he does not think to think, and where he rejects psychoanalysis. I have often wondered how one can comment so much on Derrida's philosophy, particularly in *Prayers and Tears*, and have so little to say, if anything, on Derrida's critical relationship to the body of psychoanalytic theory, from his early "Mystic Writing Pad" and even "*Différance*" to the more recent writings on Lacan. There are, in fact, several pages in Caputo's nearly 400-page volume that comment on Derrida's reading of Freud's "Jewish science," in which there is even the announcement that "Freud is the Father of us all today," but I also find it interesting that the section in which Freud's ghost is allowed to say something in response to Yerushalmi ends with the statement that "there would be no future without repetition, without the death drive to kill off the proper name of the patri-archival authority."[20] In particular, I find this statement interesting in that the act of killing off the proper name repeats, knowingly or unknowingly, the repression of the proper name of the historical Moses that was at the center of the theory that Freud put forward in *Moses and Monotheism*.

Finally, I must confess that I have always been mystified by this exclusion for the most part of the problems and concepts Derrida has drawn from the psychoanalytic field, which are dispatched to the realm of unthinkability, and that I have indeed perceived this as symptomatic and an object of repression on Caputo's part. Of course, Caputo is not alone in this, since it pertains to a certain tradition of phenomenology and hermeneutics that has evolved in the discipline of continental philosophy in North America, particularly in professional societies like the Society of Phenomenological and Existential Philosophy, which Caputo belongs to. This may be characteristic only of a particularly Anglo-American reception of Derrida's total body of work (the representation of which might be likened to a stool with only two legs). Yet I find this exclusion highly significant and almost structurally determinate of the institution of deconstruction in the United States as it has evolved since the early 1980s. If, therefore, I have been orchestrating a little play around the "return of the repressed" in my discussion of Caputo's God, particularly around the notion of Love and the noticeable absence of the sexual relation in his complimentary notion of the Good, I do not intend this in a vulgar sense of saying something like: "Jack, get thee to analysis!" I am not even announcing, in the form of a return statement, a "Return to Freud" (or Lacan for that matter). Rather, all I am saying is something like the following: "go back and read Derrida once more and have the courage *to think* what you dared to send off into unthinkability." In other words, "Repent! Sinner!" But in all seriousness, and in "the final analysis," I am also suggesting, with a little too much humor thrown in perhaps, that what we need most today is a little less religion – well, actually a lot less in my view! – and a bit more good old-time psychoanalytic pessimism; which is to say, a little less exaltation of a position of "non-knowledge" concerning the impossibility of Love, and a bit more knowledge of the hatred that binds us to this God who murders us daily, but who leaves us in the dark concerning the secret source of his passion.

Notes

A previous version of this statement appeared as "Against Religion (without Religion): A New Rationalist Reply to John D. Caputo," *Journal of Cultural and Religious Theory* 5:2 (April 2004).

1   Wright died on March 25, 1980.
2   Silko and Wright, *The Delicacy and Strength of Lace*, p. 41.
3   Ibid., pp. 45–6.

4   Freud, *Civilization and its Discontents*, p. 132.
5   See Caputo, *On Religion*, pp. 136–9.
6   Ibid.
7   Caputo, *Against Ethics*, p. 41.
8   Caputo, *On Religion*, p. 71.
9   Tina Turner, *Private Dancer*, Capital Records, 1984. If I actually took the time and care to "deconstruct" Caputo's text – Caputo's text is infinitely deconstructable – I would not begin with the title, which is a false decoy that Caputo has left for those who might argue with him. Rather, I would land on precisely what he identifies as "New Age religion." Almost all the passages against what Caputo labels as "New Age religion and popular psychology" involve dismissals of either its lukewarm, "egotistic" quality or its "poppycock" and "bizarre excesses." In other words, the grounds for dismissal regard either its lack of excess in regard to passion for the "torrents of love," or its excess of passion for superstitious beliefs. In either case, it appears to lack the proper passion of excess in the "Love of God." Here, I will simply quote the following passages from *On Religion* where this attack is most explicitly stated, often without defining what is meant by "New Age," as if this phrase had much meaning outside the decade of the 1970s in the United States, which makes me wonder if Caputo's adversary is something of a straw man and his argument somewhat dated:

1. But there is no merit in loving moderately, up to a certain point, just so far, all while watching out for number one (which is, alas, what we are often advised by a decadent "New Age" psychology). (4)
2. We live in a world where the most sophisticated and high-tech achievements co-habit not only with traditional religion but also with the most literal minded fundamentalisms, New Age spiritualities, and the belief in all sorts of bizarre, hocus-pocus phenomena. (70)
3. If God is a deed, not a thought, then that puts in perspective and gives us a way of sorting through the non-sense that is readily available in any Barnes and Noble store or on the Amazon.com website in which the love of God gets confused with New Age poppycock like the Celestine prophecy, celestial visitations by angels, channelings, sightings of Elvis, UFOs or God knows what! (136)

In these passages one might detect a certain strange brew of antagonism toward American "ego psychology" (or merely simple middle-class guilt and self-hatred), mixed with Enlightenment rationality and its suspicion of superstitious beliefs systems. But I would add, concerning the assertion that these should be disqualified as true religious phenomena, that I find essentially no difference between a contemporary sighting of Elvis and the numerous sightings of the risen Christ that are detailed in the Gospels and in Acts, nor much difference between stories of alien abduction and sexual trauma and the Annunciation. Both phenomena, strictly psychological and belonging to a historical group, express the same degree of fantasy that defines them as sincere expressions of religious sentiment on the part of those who genuinely believe in their reality. Of course, I might add here in closing that Caputo's *On Religion* is readily available in any Barnes & Noble store or on Amazon.com, alongside *The Celestine Prophecy* and books on angels and any number of studies of UFOs and alien abductions.

10 Lacan, *Four Fundamental Concepts of Psychoanalysis*, p. 199.

11 Spinoza, *The Ethics*, p. 193.

12 Lacan, *Feminine Sexuality*, p. 160.

13 Bataille, *On Nietzsche*, p. 31.

14 Spinoza, *The Ethics*, p. 198.

15 Lacan, *Four Fundamental Concepts of Psychoanalysis*, p. 200.

16 Bataille, *On Nietzsche*, p. 32.

17 Caputo, *The Prayers and Tears of Jacques Derrida*, p. 331.

18 Ibid., p. 332.

19 See Spinoza, *Theological-Political Treatise*, chapter 1, "On Signs in Prophecy."

20 Caputo, *The Prayers and Tears of Jacques Derrida*, p. 273.

3

Noli mi tangere!

A central theme of Derrida's *On Touching, Jean-Luc Nancy* is the logic of the touch, which Derrida calls "haptology."[1] The term is derived from Husserl's *Ideas II*, concerning the phenomenological sense of the *haptique*, which can be described as an elision of the usual privilege accorded to the visual sense, as well as of the transcendence implied by the dominance of the visual organ.[2] This privilege is ontologically the condition of a politics that is ruled by the visible organization of the body (*le corps*) along a vertical axis. On the other hand, perhaps the left one, the organization of the body around the privilege of "the touch" is purported to be thoroughly Christian, and lies at the heart of the doctrine of incarnation. As Jean-Luc Nancy writes in *The Deconstruction of Christianity*, "at the heart of Christianity is the doctrine of incarnation, and … at the heart of the doctrine of incarnation is the doctrine of *homoousia*, consubstantiality, the identity or community of being and substance between the father and the son."[3] Following this series of prepositional phrases, which go to the heart of the heart of the Christian doctrine, is the doctrine of the consubstantiality of father and son. Here, one can trace the passage of the semen, which bypasses a body that is touched (in the sense of being tainted or contaminated) by sexual difference.

This is an old story, so I don't have to go into it in much depth. However, one wonders if the body is touched at all, but merely irradiated, to prevent it from being tainted or mixed-up with another body. We might imagine here a process, graphically portrayed in the early Christian literature, in which the Father's semen passes through his own body, directly commingling with the body of the son, like the egg breaking apart in the yolk, so that they are of the same substance. In fact, it does not have to pass from his own body at all, which would imply a moment of *expropriation*, so that the Father's substance must then be reappropriated by the son. Of course, this would expose the Father to death. The solution of the early Church Fathers, as we know, was to figure out a way for the substance of the Father and the son to be identical; hence, there was no need for generation, for the son to be generated by or through another being, which would presuppose another generation (*genos*), or a prior genesis of substance and materiality. Needless to say, there is more than a scent of Gnosticism present in this early Christian doctrine of incarnation; at least, there is a fear of the touch passing between the Father and the son, of a kind of contact that would cause the community to become mixed up, confused, contaminated or polluted. Moreover, it is around this fear of touching and of being touched, as well as this untouchable mark of a prohibition against a certain kind of touch that passes between the Father and the son, that we find the location of the body of woman in the early Christian community. She marks, both at once, the site of touching and the fear of being touched, and her body is determined by this extreme contradiction: that is, between a body that is open to the touch and a body that is determined by the prohibition against touching.

Historically, this moment of extreme contradiction in the doctrine of incarnation locates the body of woman and is produced by the social and religious codes of purity and pollution that belonged to the societies of that time. It is reported in Mark 16:1 that Mary Magdalene and Mary the mother of James went to the tomb with spices to anoint the body of Jesus. In other words, they went to touch and handle a corpse, which was first of all an act that pollutes and contaminates – that enfranchises the boundary between the living and the dead, between living body and corpse, or dead animal hide – but one that somehow was open to these two women. In Matthew 28:1 it is said to be Mary Magdalene and simply "the other Mary" who visit the tomb. In Luke 23:55 through 24:12, it is Mary Magdalene, Joanna, Mary the mother of James, and "certain other women" (who are not identified in this account) who go to prepare the corpse with "spices and fragrant oils." In John, it is just Mary Magdalene, and it is here that Jesus' statement to Mary is added: "Do not touch me, for I have not yet ascended to the Father." By contrast, In Matthew 28:9, the women hold onto the feet of the resurrected Jesus and worship him, which is why the Greek is sometimes translated as "to cling" rather than to touch. This might also be interpreted as the Gospel writer's message to the early Christian community he is addressing: "stop clinging to my body," perhaps even in the sense of preventing the body of the Christ from becoming a mere fetish. "I am not there," we might hear Jesus saying to Mary Magdalene, who could very well represent a certain sect of the early Christian community who might be "clinging" to the idea of the bodily resurrection of Christ.

In *Corpus* (2000), Nancy addresses the problem of the body around this tactile image. What Nancy calls the body's "other sense" must be distinguished from the body's superficial sense (*res extensia*), that is, the body wholly determined from "the outside," whose surface can be touched, whose parts and members can be cut or segmented, scarred or tattooed, colored or translucent, adorned or profaned. It is this sense of the body that we usually refer to when we say "the body" or "my body" since it is first of all open to perception, including the tactile perception of the touch, and consequently to signification as well. It is this sense of the body, as a matter of the *sign*, that is open to the kind of touch that leaves an indelible trace or mark of a sign that is interposed, or that sticks to the body (as in the sign of race or ethnicity, or the sign of voluptuousness, or it's the lack thereof in the sense we talk today of "hard bodies"). However, this sense must be radically opposed to another, more absolute, sense of the body that cannot be identified (or rather "recognized") among the various senses by which the body is determined or signified as in the above examples. Nancy names this opposition of two senses the "antinomy of the body," wherein what is found to be proper to the body is always crossed through and divided by this antinomy.[4]

According to this antinomy, the origin of "the spirit" can be understood to derive from this "other body," as a shadow cast from the sense of a body that remains *in every sense* a stranger to the body defined by its external senses (sensations including "touch," perception, image, memory, idea, and consciousness). As Nancy argues, it is precisely on the basis of this living contradiction that the famous dualism of the philosophical tradition unfolds, from Descartes and Hegel all the way through to Sartre and Merleau-Ponty, in which the body is expressed in some fashion as the "obstacle to sense" or where the "Sense of sense" is inextricably bound up with the existential experience of our own bodies.[5] The question I will pose later on, in the context of the Gospels, is whether the sense of this other body should immediately be identified with the body of woman, or whether there is yet another body that precedes even this one, that is, the body marked by sexual difference, and of "one sex" in particular; and, finally, whether it is from this other body that *the sense of the body of woman unfolds* as a problem that marks both the origin and the extreme limit of what Nancy refers to as "our tradition" (i.e., Christianity, or "*christianisme*" [*sic*])?

For the moment, in order to illustrate further the two opposing senses of the body, we might find this distinction at the origin of the body's concealed surfaces – the privation of the visibility of its sexual parts, for example – as if, in these locations, the body's superficial and extended sense turns inward and approaches the sense of the body's inner sense, that is, the privation of this outward and external sense of the body. These zones of privation and concealment (invisibility) are literally created or produced when a portion of the body's surface is folded back, creating an enclave or cryptic enclosure that is confused with the body's inner sense. And yet, the interior of these folds remain located on the outside of the body, they literally appear *on* the body, even though they are bound up with a privation of the merely superficial sense of the body's other surfaces (for example, the surface of my forearm, or calf, or the stretch of the body that runs along my back, or my forehead – and it is interesting that the Latin compound words in English that commonly refer to these portions of the body are usually indicated as being "foreword" or "up front," of being a side that in some way "faces").[6] The fact that these folded and cryptically interior portions of the body's surface are the effects of this function of privation, that they are confused and mixed

71

up with the body's other sense, can be easily demonstrated by the uncanny quality that surrounds the visibility of the body's orifices, and not only the so-called sexual orifices, but also the cavity of the mouth, the nostrils, the ears, or even the eyes. This is particularly true when these orifices appear too close to us – for example, while kissing someone I might focus on one eye, which suddenly appears to me as grotesque, as a yawning cavity – and, thus, no longer remain in the background, as parts set peacefully into the exterior composition of a face or a head.

Given these observations, one wonders if the sexually determined orifices are, in fact, *a posteriori* to this other sense of the body, that is, the metonymically organized effects or the expressions of what Nancy calls the absolute "For-Itself" of the body's own "auto-symbolization." As Nancy writes, "*The* body is nothing less than *the auto-symbolization of an absolute organ*."[7] If we could perform a phenomenological "reduction" (*epoché*) of the positive attributes that define these exterior-interior zones of the body's surface in psychological and moral representations, we would of course quickly discover that they have undergone (and continue to undergo) a seemingly infinite number of variations between cultures and historical periods, and are even exposed to different vicissitudes on an individual level in the psychoanalytic sense of perversion. This is why I referred to them above as metonymically organized, in order to call attention to the fact that we are speaking about the organization of significations here and not about the body In-Itself. In fact, we might discover them to be the purest expressions of the manner in which the two senses of the body are folded, or in which these senses are confused on the body's surface, causing the over-all *Gestalt* (or image) of the body to be shaped, contorted, deformed around the absolute tension, perhaps even the violent contraction,

72

between the infinite openness of the body (to perception, representation, or signification, and touch), and a sense that opposes these predicates of the body's openness, expressing instead an aspect of imperceptibility in which the body remains, to all the senses, untouchable.

We might imagine that these folded points function as vortices in the body – Nancy himself refers to them as "black holes" – and the effects of distortion they produce could be similar to the organization of the body in the paintings of Francis Bacon, where the body is visibly pulled and pushed around certain opaque points in the center of the composition (although it is important to note that these points never appear visibly, only the distorting effects of their presence). What I have been describing above, of course, has been metaphorically represented in the psychoanalytic theory of the mirror stage as the phallic moment of "mis-recognition" that splits the Subject into pure façade and the formless presence of the body's drives that subsequently causes the subject to suffer from "feelings of fragmentation." However, precisely because it is a metaphorical representation, this psychoanalytic image of the mirror stage must be bracketed as well, since it is already a signification that responds to the hypothesis concerning the origin of a particular formation of the ego's bodily image. In *Corpus,* Nancy writes:

> The body is the Living Temple – the life as Temple and the temple as Living, the one touching the other as a sacred mystery – only by achieving absolutely the circularity that founds it. It is necessary that sense be embodied, in itself and eternally, for the body to make sense – and reciprocally. Thus, the sense of "sense" is bodily, and the sense of the "body" is sensed. Within this circular re-absorption of sense, any established signification is immediately wiped away ... The body is the organ of sense,

that is, the organ (or *organon*), absolutely (one can also say here: the system, the community, the communion, the subjectivity, the finality, etc.). The body is, therefore, nothing less than the auto-symbolization of the absolute organ. Unnamable as God, never exposed to an exterior understanding ... unnamable in addition to comprising an intimate texture-of-self towards which every philosophy of the "body proper" exhausts itself ("what we call the flesh, this internally worked over matter, nameless in any philosophy" – Merleau-Ponty). God, Death, and Flesh: the trinity of every onto-theology. The body is an exhaustive combinatory, the common assumption of these three impossible names, before which all signification trembles.[8]

Because of this absolute sense accorded to the body as a circularity without foundation, this "For-Itself" and "In-Itself" that defines the body – which, most importantly, can be said to be actual moments of sense that belong to our experience of own bodies (as well as the bodies of others) – Nancy provides a philosophical justification for understanding why the body would become an expression of divinity in "*our tradition*," meaning our Christian tradition founded upon the doctrine of the incarnation of the sacred in the body of an individual.

I would like to underscore the significance of Nancy's statement for interpreting the status of Christian onto-theology, which in some sense also encompasses the onto-theology of the West. What we call the body, for better or worse, is the common locus or source for the three impossible experiences of the "In-Itself" and the "For-Itself," in short, for three experiences of an Absolute Inside. Of course, these are not experiences properly speaking, since we cannot "traverse" them, go "beyond" or "outside" of them; as Nancy writes, they constitute a sense before which every signification lapses into nothingness. Therefore, it is the historical and onto-theological characteristic of "*our tradition*" to have consecrated this sense with a form of the sacred, and to have filled it with an experience of mystery and terror. From this moment onward, the body will be positioned as the nexus of these three impossible names: God, Death, and the Living Flesh. (For this last impossible name, I might simply prefer Life, or Life-in-itself, which might be a better translation of *Leib* in order to avoid the archaic moral signification that is attached to the word "Flesh".) Thus, it is in this sense of the word that I sense my body as a "circularity without ground," as a living absolute whose finality excludes me. If Nancy refers to this circularity as the "auto-symbolization of an absolute organ," this is because Life makes sense in or with my body in a manner that absolutely excludes any relation to my consciousness or the ego. That is to say, consciousness does not exist as either a moment of this circulation, or as its end – its relation is always outside or exterior to the relation between the body and life. Therefore, from this moment onward, the body will be the common site of these three names, up to and including this current moment in secular culture where the body is located as the privileged locus of identity and freedom of the sexual subject. I pause to ask, can we imagine a moment outside or beyond "our tradition" that is, beyond a Christian onto-theological "humanism" (as Derrida has described our epoch)? If so, then perhaps it would be precisely when our bodies wouldn't matter.[9] In short, perhaps "the body" is the name of the most powerful trope introduced by Christianity; the body is a "tropological organism" *par excellence*, already installed as the most primitive articulation of flesh and language, from which every performativity of the flesh (from conversion to sexuation) derives its absolute sense of "auto-symbolization."

Nancy's statement concerning the trinity (God, Death, and Flesh) can be interpreted to mean that Christianity makes

Death a divine name, just as much as it makes Life a form of the divine – but that wouldn't be too different from other religious systems either, in terms of the divinity of Life or of Death. What is specific to the Christian transformation of the divine is neither Death nor Life, nor even the figure of a God, but rather the incarnation of all three senses of the divine within the sense of the body. Henceforth, the sense of the body is inextricably bound up with the senses of these divine names. Death is not identical with abstract death, which, as Hegel said, was like the toppling of a pile of sand, but rather with the dead body. Life is no longer Life, but the living body, life embodied. Returning to the end of the Gospels, it is significant to note that all three names are thoroughly implicated in what could be called the *parousia* of the new divinity announced by the early Christian religion. In the tomb scene we have an event that is first of all bodily, present in the flesh; that is, the emphasis is placed on an experience that took on a form of contact with a living body. As I noted above, the form of this contact (between Mary and Jesus) could take place outside the social and moral-juridical prohibitions that gave rise to it and made it both normative and exceptional at the same time.

A woman (or "certain women") goes to a tomb, a place of death (*loculus*, a burial chamber in a tomb), and finds a living body. Once again, I stress the importance of the fact that the laws governing contact already make it possible for women to enter into this place, to come into contact with death, even if they will be surprised at what they find. This would imply that this experience, and thus everything that happens to them, was only possible on the basis of the fact that their bodies were already determined to be open to coming into contact with death, to touching the dead. Concerning the revelation of divinity, or *parousia*, the presence of the divine, I would not place as much emphasis on the poetic and allegorical elements of the accounts – the appearance of the "youth" (*neaniskos*) in Mark, or even of the living body of the resurrected Christ in the later synoptic Gospels and the Gospel of John – as on the reactions of the women to what they witness. In Mark, it is said they are "stunned," *eklambestha*, which is also translated as "utterly amazed," or "remaining in a stupor," perhaps implying that the sense of what they witnessed at that moment remained with them for some time, like a shadow that caused the sense of what they experienced to remain strange, if not a cause of their estrangement. Of course, the earliest Gospel ends by reinforcing this reaction. I will translate it literally: They ran away, possessed by trembling (*tromos*) and confusion (*ekstasis*), saying nothing to anybody (*oudeni ouden*). In Matthew, the women's first reaction is described simply as one of "fear" (*phobos*), and they are even told that "they need not be afraid" (Matthew 28:5). In John, most interestingly, Mary does not even recognize Jesus at first (literally, she does not comprehend what she sees presented to her in body and flesh), not until Jesus calls her by name and she responds in the Aramaic, "My Master" (*Rabboni*). In all these passages, what is revealed is sensed without receiving a clear significa-tion; in each case, the signification refers back to the sense of the experience, which is fear, trembling, confusion, amazement, stupor, and miscomprehension (all words that refer their sense primarily to the body, or express the body's relation to an event), which also might imply that the revelation of the divine has a sense that is primarily addressed to the body, which implies an indirect relation to conscious recognition or understanding.

It is clear that what we have here closely corresponds to what Nancy describes as an experience before which all signification trembles. But this trembling does not concern the neutral or neutered body, of male *and* female, which does not exist; so we must return to ask: where does the sexed body figure in Nancy's account of "our tradition"? When we situate the above schema of the two contradictory senses of the body in the context of social and moral representations, we find a more accurate and revealing portrait of how this tension receives signification and content. These significations are not distributed evenly among all bodies, of course; rather, this tension appears more forcefully to mark some bodies than others. This is particularly true in the case of sexual difference, and as I noted above the body of woman is socially defined by the contrasting tension of openness (voluptuousness) and by moral prohibition, which is especially remarked in the figure of Mary Magdalene.

According to popularized Christian legend, the body of Mary Magdalene was full of semen, awash with the touch of other bodies. For this reason she incarnates the limit of the touchable, which turns around the prohibition that defines her social class and that of "certain other women." We might ask ourselves – and we would certainly not be the first to raise this question – why the synoptic Gospels constantly underscore the encounter between Mary Magdalene and the figure of the resurrected Christ (represented by the *neaniskos* in the Gospel of Mark) as the meeting of the two extremes of the prohibitions concerning touch: the expression of the two senses of untouchable. I have thus far only counted two, but there are actually three senses of the untouchable in the ending of the Gospels: the untouchable that defines Mary, according to popular Christian mythology, to belong to the class of prostitutes; the untouchable that defines the body of Jesus as a dead carcass, a corpse, or cadaver, and; third, the untouchable that appears in the Gospel of John, which concerns the prohibition on touching the resurrected and yet unsanctified body of the Christ. I have not counted the third only because it might be considered an aberration belonging to the Neo-Platonism of the fourth Gospel, or at least a didactic and moral moment that the Gospel writer is addressing to the Johannian community. (Perhaps it concerns certain fetishistic practices or beliefs that have developed concerning the body of Christ. In this sense, I would read it as similar to the injunction we find in Matthew: "stop clinging to me," that is, stop fetishizing my body.[10])

In general, I tend to read the significance of the different versions of the tomb narrative very explicitly along the lines of their common theme (addressed to instruct the intended audiences – who were after all, at least for the most part, fairly simple folk), which is: stop looking for me in the tomb, since I am not there. Stop looking for my body among the dead, because it is a "living body." The Gospel writers, as teachers, wouldn't want to confound their students; this task falls to scholars and academics in the centuries that follow, a group that could be classified as a crowd of "bad students." According to the Christian testament scholar, Herman Waetjen, this judgment can even be found in the portrait of the original disciples, particularly in the Gospel of Mark, who as a band come off looking like "blockheads." Yet, it is the conversion of Mary Magdalene (perhaps a representative of the untouchable classes) into a living member of the early Christian community that receives its allegorical representation in the conversion of a corpse into a living person. According to the scholarship surrounding the social position of women in early Christian communities, she represents the extreme principle of inversion that defined the *ethos* of the early Christian sects: the incarnation of all the untouchable classes in one body (or community), the reversal and abolition of existing purity codes, whereby the bodies of those who were defined outside the limits of contact are incorporated into a new community whose inaugurating principle is the transgression of this prohibition surrounding touching that shaped the former social and moral order. According to the thesis of Schüssler-Fiorenza, Mary can therefore be identified as the first apostle ("the apostle to the apostles," or the mother to the church fathers, so to speak), the true witness of the resurrection and the life of Jesus, who lived afterwards in fear of Roman persecution and death, a radical Christian, a *mater familias*.[11] But then, this conversion has had profound repercussions; the canceling of the prohibitions surrounding touch, that is, the conversion of the untouchable into a principle of contact and community, definitely played havoc in early Christian societies, and does so even today, between the body defined by sexual contact (*porneia*) and the "body proper" defined by Christian morality.

It is only later, as what historian Wayne A. Meeks has defined as a fundamental ambiguity in early Christianity (and particularly with the ascendance of Pauline Christianity), that the principle of extreme openness that marked many of the early Christian sects is brought into tension with Greco-Roman social mores and class distinctions, mostly those belonging to the upper classes.[12] It is no accident, then, that throughout the history of Christian societies this confusion continued to be expressed in the ambivalence and extreme contradictions that determine (socially, morally, and even philosophically) the bodies of women. As Paul wrote, "It is good for a person not to touch a woman" (1 Cor. 7:1). I might even go further and say that the body of woman is engendered to incarnate this extreme division that belongs to the body in general, even to the degree that she is made entirely responsible for it, and that it is this spirit of hatred (misogyny) that underscores almost all the early treatments of the division of the sexes in the writings of Paul, Philo, Aquinas, and Constantine. This history can be understood as the expression of an extreme "ambivalence" (Meeks) that has shaped both the determination of the body's sexuality and the representation of woman in later Christian societies, including our own. If feminism has emerged most forcefully in our century, then perhaps it represents a political body (a community) that was already prefigured in the fateful meeting of Mary and Jesus. In this encounter we already bear witness to a volatile principle of community founded upon the contradiction between touch and the untouchable, in other words, between inclusion and exclusion. Insofar as Christianity remains "our tradition," it is this same principle of extreme opposition that continues to haunt every representation of the "political body" today.[13] At the same time, the political significance that has been recently accorded to the body in "our tradition" is in some ways already redundant. As Nancy reminds us, "'the political body' is already a tautology."[14]

Notes

A previous version of this statement appeared as "Untouchable," in Kevin Hart and Yvonne Sherwood (eds), *Derrida and Religion: Other Testaments* (London: Routledge, 2004), pp. 415–31.

1   Derrida, *On Touching: Jean-Luc Nancy*, pp. 174ff.
2   Cited in ibid., pp. 196ff.
3   Nancy, "La deconstruction du christianisme," cited in Derrida, *Le Toucher: Jean-Luc Nancy*, p. 273.
4   Nancy, *Corpus*, pp. 71ff.
5   Ibid., p. 61.

6 Derrida has commented on this Latin root in relation to the psychoanalytic theory of introjection, or cryptonomy, in "Fors," his preface to Abraham and Torok's *The Wolf Man's Magic Word: Cryptonomy*.

7 Nancy, *Corpus*, p. 64.

8 Ibid., pp. 66–7.

9 The above reference, of course, is to Judith Butler's *Bodies That Matter*, which according to the above argument could be said to belong to a Christian onto-theological humanism in that it defines the body as an "In-Itself" converted into a "For-Itself," that is, a self-consciousness that transforms the body into a privileged site its own auto-symbolization (i.e., "performativity").

10 Waetjen, *A Reordering of Power*, pp. 149–64.

11 Schüssler-Fiorenza, *In Memory of Her*, p. 333.

12 Meeks, "Since Then You Would Need to Go Out Into the World," pp. 4–29.

13 Nancy, *Corpus*, p. 64.

14 Ibid.

4

"… tacitly, the caress, in a word, the Christian body"

Before continuing my investigation of the presence of a certain implicit and presupposed "theological turn" in continental philosophy, I want to return again to make a preliminary cautionary remark concerning what is already implicated in the very designation of a "theological turn," particularly in the context of the post-Heideggerian tradition of phenomenology. As I stated in the introduction, this designation has a quasi-mythic significance that has overdetermined the purely conceptual meaning of "turning" or "reversal" (*die Kehre*), and has provided a "paradigm" in which the contemporary relationship between theology and phenomenology appears already predestined. In other words, just as in the case of many other "return statements" (linguistic, cultural, anthropological, communitarian), the "theological turn" would be an "instance" of a general class of argumentation for which Heidegger's *die Kehre* would provide the model or theoretical paradigm, in the sense that Kuhn outlined with regard to what he called "normal scientific research."[1] This paradigm – which, I would immediately add, has received its most paradigmatic expression in the recent writings of Jean-Luc Nancy – rather than signaling the abandonment of "pure phenomenology" or simply the reversal of an earlier scientific paradigm, signals instead the emergence of specifically theological (that is, fundamentally "Christian") concepts and themes in phenomenological thinking today. This constitutes the completion of what was previously attempted strictly according to an earlier understanding of the phenomenological method. Ironically, and against many of the overt statements of its founding practitioners,[2] it is the theological content that today provides a necessary "corrective" to an earlier scientific prejudice (or "rationalism"). Here I am thinking especially of Heidegger's claim in his 1927 lecture "Phenomenology and Theology" that phenomenology functions as a corrective to the basic concepts employed by theology: "Philosophy is the possible, formally indicative ontological corrective of the ontic and, in particular, of the pre-Christian content of basic theological concepts."[3]

However, according to the new return statement, this would have be to rephrased as follows: "Theology is the possible, implicitly ontological corrective of the pre-scientific content of basic (post)modern philosophical concepts." In other words, again, according to a paradigmatic (even "performative") understanding of the "theological turn in phenomenology," one that is prevalent among many philosophers today (including Nancy and Agamben), what was implicit was already destined *to become* explicit; therefore, it expresses the character of an essence and should not be understood as an extraneous and accidental phenomenon, i.e., *per accidens*. In the following, I will attempt to bracket this determination of what is "implicit" (if not presupposed), but not in the sense of immediately relegating the theological to a purely extraneous instance in the history of the phenomenological tradition. Instead – and here I will be primarily referring to Derrida's "reading" of a "certain French

84

tradition of phenomenology" in *Le Toucher: Jean-Luc Nancy* – I would like to propose a more complicated *topology* of what is implicated in the contemporary relationship between theology and phenomenology (and, of course, philosophy more generally). In fact, the entire argument of *Le Toucher* is underscored by a gesture of finger pointing; and it seems that by being "faithful" to Derrida's own reading I am also implicated in this gesture, even in the act of pointing it out in Derrida's text. Nevertheless, the main point of Derrida's original gesture does not remain simply at the level of a pun on the word hand (*main*), but rather points to the implicit "anthropocentric privilege" of the human hand (and, therefore, of caressing, or touching) in the history of the phenomenological tradition itself, beginning with Husserl and Heidegger, to whom I will return later on.

First, however, I would like to outline the multiple senses of the implicit that are already present in Derrida's argument concerning, ultimately, what he will later come to identify as a specifically "Christian thinking of the flesh." The first sense of the implicit, of course, concerns the phenomenological tradition being understood from something else that remains unexpressed, or at least not "explicitly avowed," namely French Catholicism. In pointing out this sense of what is implicit in the tradition of phenomenology in France, beginning with Merleau-Ponty, Derrida confesses to an "impertinent pertinence" in participating from the perspective of a stranger.[4] Ironically, here Derrida will not only include those philosophers who could be explicitly linked to this position of faith, but will also refer to others who would at first sight seem to be affiliated as disciples, namely to the different trajectories of Levinas and Nancy. It is precisely through the thematic of "the caress" – "tacitly, the caress, in a word, the Christian body" – that both of these trajectories are related and participate within "a certain tradition of French phenomenology." As Derrida writes:

> One day, together and separately, one will indeed have to reread these two thinking approaches to the caress, Levinas' and Nancy's, and from the outset follow this theme within each of their trajectories, more particularly in order to pinpoint their respective differences in relation to phenomenology, beyond the discrepancies that keep them apart.[5]

"Furthermore," he writes: "there may be a religious fund that the two thinkers share (*partage*) in more ways than would at first seem. Levinas sometimes plays a game ... he plays at confessing a Catholicism that Nancy, for his part, seriously disclaims."[6]

If only by implication, what Derrida is pointing to here in both passages addresses the second sense of the implicit mathematically defined as an expression in which one or more independent variables are not separated on opposite sides of an equation. In this case, if the major argument of *Le Toucher* is the critique of "intuitionism" found in the French phenomeno-logical tradition, beginning with Merleau-Ponty, then what might first appear to be the exact opposite of this tradition (i.e., what might be called an "anti-intuitionist phenomenology," or a phenomenological gesture that would be non-intuitionist in principle, namely, the principle of "non-substitution"), would, in fact, appear on the same side of the equation. It is at this point that Derrida recounts the story (*histoire*) of a contingent history of a "manifold tradition" that would necessarily include all bifurcations and opposing points of view; elsewhere, he refers to "the manifold tradition, at the crossroads of filiations or trends both heterogeneous and affined, from Maine de Biran ... to Merleau-Ponty *and Gilles Deleuze*, by way (of course) of

Husserl's *Ideas II*."[7] Moreover, all of these different trajectories touch on a crucial passage from Husserl's *Ideas II* on the haptic principle; consequently, from this point onward they would constitute altogether *one tangent*. In other words, the "tangent" is the precise scheme that Derrida employs to unite all these different trajectories, which could be compared to curves or folds in the flesh, at a certain point where they all run together in a straight line, in the sense of sharing (*partage*) the same tangent.

So, we might ask, "what's the point"? And what does this have to do with "the implicit and presupposed theological turn of phenomenology"? In fact, this will be strictly derivative, in Derrida's reading, from a certain "anthropological privilege (sometimes unavowed)," which is already implicit in Husserlian phenomenology. Such a privilege is expressed in three different manners: First, in the reduction of the relation of the world to only pertain to human beings (implicitly, referring to the Heideggerian concept of *Mitsein*). Second, "in the neglect of what is not human flesh," including the flesh of animals and "technological prostheses."[8] As for the third, the one that leads directly on a path to a "Christian thinking of the flesh," I will simply quote the passage in which this phrase first appears, which will form the basis of my own reading. Here, Derrida writes:

> When this privilege of the human imparts itself too readily, it frees the path more easily − unless it has already entered it − toward this anthropological, or even *Christian, thinking of the flesh, tactility, the caress, in a word, the Christian body*, which I am not trying to denounce or reject here, but to "think" − i.e., to "ponder," or to "weigh."[9]

The question this passage raises is the following: does the anthropological privilege that is already implicitly present in

Husserl's phenomenological reduction of the world to the limits of the human ego (although in a manner that is "sometimes disavowed" by his followers) lead directly to "this Christian thinking of the flesh"? In other words, is the theological turning of phenomenology, or the turning of phenomenology into a Christian theology, already implicit in this earlier anthropo-centricism, first that of Husserl and then of Merleau-Ponty? In response, Derrida hints, this occurs when this anthropocentrism, which was already implicit in Husserlian phenomenology with the phenomenological reduction of *the human world*, "imparts itself too readily" on the path toward a thinking of the flesh (in the sense of its immediacy, immanence, or even in the sense of its incarnation in the body). It would seem, therefore, that everything is contingent on how one determines the body and how easily it assumes a concept of a strictly *human flesh*. That is, it sets off on a tangent leading on its path to, "in a word, *the Christian Body*." But then perhaps this raises the question of another path, another thinking of the body, that would not already be led down this path. Perhaps of another body altogether? Of course, in the reference "to one or several paths" that belong to the post-Husserlian tradition of Heideggerian phenomenology, perhaps Derrida is implicitly stating his fidelity to another path, one that diverges from a certain French tradition that has too easily set off in the direction of the body and its presupposed immediacy to the sense of existence. Otherwise, how are we to interpret the reference to those "already on the path"? Does this refer to those thinkers who are overtly religious, the so-called believers? Catholics and Christians alike?[10] Or would this also include those, like Nancy, who are already set upon a path of disclaiming their Catholicism, as well as others, like Levinas, who "play the game" of confessing themselves Catholic around certain themes that frequent the French phenomenological tradition, "tacitly, the caress"?

Instead of attempting to answer these larger questions that belong only to the context of "a certain French tradition" – one that I would say, in the sense of changing the topic of a conversation, is "all too French!" – let us now turn to the exact passage from Husserl's *Ideas II* where Derrida appears to implicate "a Christian thinking of the flesh." The passage in question, first cited at a crucial point by Merleau-Ponty in *Signs*, concerns the phenomenological reduction in the appresentation between self and other, where Husserl stipulates that while I can have access to the other person's "corporeality" (*Leiblichkeit*) only by indirect appresentation – by analogy, projection, or by "introjection" – I will never have any direct access to the incarnation of the other in her own proper body "without introjection" (*ohne Introjektion*).[11] This becomes for Husserl the dual appresentation of the other person as a unitary phenomenon: on one side, the other's *Leib* (*corps propre*) appears only indirectly by the analogy, projection, or introjection of my own sense of incarnation (for lack of a better word); on the other side, the other's own carnal "corporeality" (*Leiblichkeit*) remains "without introjection," which is to say, can never become fully incarnated in myself or as an expression of my own "bodily Consciousness" (*Leibbewusstein*). Nevertheless, as I will argue below following Derrida's own pointers, what cannot be introjected nevertheless can become "incorporated" forming a "cryptic enclosure" in the doubled but nevertheless unitary movement of the appresentation of the other person. The corporeality of the other person is included as excluded, but is nevertheless present in the double and unitary movement of consciousness. However, even though this "non-mine-ness" is part of the unitary sense of this total presentation of the other person as a phenomenon, it cannot itself be made into a form of co-presentation or co-incidence, which is to say, into a shared-divided (*partage*) experience of originary "ex-propriation." As Derrida goes on to insist in his reading of this "chiasmus," even the existential sense of "without introjection" (*ohne Introjektion*) cannot – *and, moreover, must not!* (Derrida insists on this at several points) – be made co-incident, or co-present, as if my own sense of bodily existence (which is without introjection) could become co-implicated or synchronous with the other person's expropriation of my own proper incarnation. Here, Derrida cautions, by making this very expropriation itself a form of sharing (*partage*), "one runs the risk of reconstituting an intu-itionism of immediate access to the other by means of its exact opposite," which is to say, non-coincidence, in a word, alterity.[12]

It is precisely around this last point, I believe, that we have located a third sense of what is "implicit," which, as I stated above, opens up a much more complex *topology*, one in which the other would remain *as other*, "without introjection," but at the same time would be included with the self, even if this inclusion would take the form of a pure "spacing" that remains exterior to the self and its introjections. Thus, we might return to the first sense of the implicit, concerning a religious sense that is "sometimes unavowed" – meaning unacknowledged *as such*, though not completely disavowed, but rather "cryptically avowed," or "encrypted." *Where* is this sense encrypted? Again: "tacitly, in the caress, in a word, the Christian body." Since I am claiming to be "faithful" to Derrida's own reading of this passage, let me explicitly state what I am suggesting here: that what is described above in terms of a fundamental non-disclosure of the sense of corporeality (precisely, of the other's bodily sense of incarnation) in the appresentation of the other person becomes thematized in Derrida's own reading under the psychoanalytic notion of "cryptic incorporation," particularly with regard to the phenomenological themes of the caress and of the touch. In other words, Derrida seems to identify a similar structure, or logic of incorporation, that also leads to what he calls a "Christian thinking of the flesh," as if providing an answer to the question of a theological phenomenology, since it appears to be structured by the same form of non-disclosure. Of course, here I am making explicit, in the sense of "making a thesis of," what Derrida himself chooses to keep implicit in his own text – for reasons that must be exposed to interpretation as well. For now, in order to provide some initial evidence for my reading, I will first point to the many allusions to the various crypts in *Le Toucher*, beginning with the very first "tangent" on the passage from Nancy's *Corpus* (2000) concerning the figure of Psyche who is "extended in her coffin" asleep, as if dead, before Eros who contemplates her.[13] Moreover, we must recognize that Derrida's own commentary on these allusions is equally "cryptic" or "elliptical," as if attempting to avoid any explicit statement or explanation. In other words, the appearance of the crypt remains strictly at the level of the figure, which is also extended to include the different figures of secrecy and the cipher that would need to be deciphered according to the method of "cryptonomy." What could this mean?

In risking a preliminary interpretation – before I have even attempted to find the key or cipher – I would first of all suggest that the "Christian body" (or any "Christian thinking of the flesh" for that matter) could only exist as a foreign body in Derrida's own text. In fact, Derrida seems to go to incredible lengths in maintaining a certain distance from the very citations he includes in the body of his own text, particularly in the case of the citations from Nancy's *Corpus*, as if dramatizing their exteriority from his own position or point of view; perhaps even in the sense of *not wanting to get mixed up with this particular body*, of getting "con-fused," which ultimately leads to a series of gestures all of which can be understood as acts of distancing himself from Nancy's *Corpus*, that is, as the pointed attempts to read this body without touching it, or what it "implicitly" contains. For example, I provide the following example of a preamble to a citation of Nancy's text that exhibits, to an almost contortion-ist degree, the rhetorical gesture to which I refer here: "Here, so as to limit the risks of an appropriating interpretation and demonstrate more clearly, down to the letter, the way in which Nancy does what he says, and writes and incorporates what he thinks into ex-scribing, here is a second passage from *Corpus*."[14] I am calling attention here not only to the superficial character-istics of Derrida's own manner of "touching" Nancy's text, but also to the manner in which he constantly draws attention to the very status of "reading" as a method, technique, or procedure of incorporating bits and portions of another body of writing, or the so-called primary text (*partes extra partes*), into another discourse and, in this case, *into Derrida's own proper body*. In other words, if Derrida's usual procedure of "reading" has usually gone by the name of deconstruction, in this case the procedure (or method) that appears to govern his approach to another body of writing, particularly the writing of Jean-Luc Nancy, seems more to approximate a method of cryptonomy. The difference between so-called "normal reading" (the method of hermeneutic discernment of the author's intentionality, or even a decon-structive strategy that calls into question the normal protocols) and the technique of reading that is implied by a cryptonomy concerns the status of a certain unconscious significance that operates throughout the so-called primary text, a significance that is fashioned artificially in order to keep the contents of what this text discloses hidden, or to maintain by means of encrypting or ciphering what is overtly being communicated.[15]

Beyond the merely superficial effects or external signs of something cryptic operating in this text, I will return to make explicit the logic of "incorporation" which moreover occurs "beyond the limit of introjection" in order to decipher Derrida's own use of this concept in relation to the crucial passage from Husserl's *Ideas II* discussed above. The topic (*topos*) of the crypt first appears in Derrida's earlier foreword to Nicolas Abraham's and Maria Torok's *Cryptonomie: Le verbier de L'Homme aux loups* (1976), and primarily concerns the technical distinction between the meta-psychological concepts of introjection and incorporation. First, the self is defined as "the set of all introjections" that includes all objects (others) as well as the instincts and desires that are attached to them. Succinctly phrased, according to Ferenczi's definition of introjection, "insofar as he loves an object, he adopts it as a part of his Self."[16] What is defined as "incorporation" only occurs in exceptional cases and certain limit situations (especially in the limit situation that interrupts the process of normal mourning) when an introjected loved-object is lost followed by the demand that the self undergo libidinal reorganization; that is to say, according to Torok's rigorous redefinition of the concept, incorporation only occurs at the limits of introjection itself, and "when introjection, for some reason, fails."[17] This failure, amounting to a rejection and even a "foreclosure" of so-called normal mourning (what Torok calls a "*maladie de deuil*" or "mourning sickness"), results in the creation of a "cryptic enclave" (an outside, *foris*) within the self where the object is "saved" as Other (i.e., as a heterogeneous and foreign body encrypted in the self, which we have already defined following Ferenczi as the "set of all introjections"). In other words, the act of incorporating the loved-object (as still living, beyond death) is, in the strongest sense imaginable, *the refusal of the reality of this object's loss* (hence, the approximation to a psychotic reality), as well as representing perhaps the most "fantastic" (phantasmatic) solution to the demand for libidinal reorganization that is normally associated with death. As Derrida writes:

> Sealing the loss of the object, but also marking the refusal to mourn, such a maneuver is foreign to and actually opposed to the process of introjection [and by implication, against the very normal topology of the Self as "the set of all introjections"]. I pretend to keep the dead alive, intact, *safe (save) inside me*, but it is only in order to refuse, in a necessarily equivocal manner, to love the dead as a living part of me, dead *save in me*, through the process of introjection, as happens in so-called "Normal mourning."[18]

And immediately following the above passage:

> The most inward safe (the crypt as an artificial unconscious-ness, as the Self's artifact) becomes outcast (*Hormis*, except for, save, *fors*), the Outside (*foris*) with respect to the outer safe (the Self) that includes it without comprehending it, in order to comprehend nothing in it ... Without a doubt, the Self does identify, in order to resist introjection, but in an "imaginary and occult" manner, with the lost object, with "its life beyond the grave." ... But the inclusion is real; it is not of the order of fantasy.[19]

On the basis of these two passages from the earlier foreword on the cryptonymic logic of incorporation, we can immediately ask whether Derrida's frequent allusions to this logic in the process of "pondering and weighing" (that is, attempting to think) a specifically "Christian thinking of the flesh" might also imply the possibility of a magical operation that occurs at the limits of introjection also appearing in the passage from Husserl's *Ideas II*? In other words, the limit of introjection itself, as well as the process of incorporation that appears somehow "beyond this limit," already echoes the problem Derrida had already raised concerning "how to save the other *as* Other." As he writes in "Fors":

> Like the original boundary line, the topographical divider separating introjection from incorporation is rigorous in principle [here, in Torok's definition, or in the latter text, in Husserl's original intuition], but in fact does not rule out all sorts of original compromises [or "con-fusions," as in the case ascribed to Merleau-Ponty]. The ambiguity I mentioned earlier (the reappropriation of the other *as* other) actually makes the compromise irreducible.[20]

In my reading of this passage, I have enfolded the later argument from *Le Toucher* only to cause the problem concerning an original, and it seems, irreducible "equivocation" between the two senses of introjection and incorporation to appear more explicitly. In fact, it is only in the later text that Derrida refuses any compromise with the sense of the other *as* other (that is, "beyond introjection"), and by faithfully adhering to Husserl's own principle he criticizes Merleau-Ponty for precisely exposing this principle to the worst con-fusion. Could not "the *ek-static* inclusion of the other's flesh" (Merleau-Ponty), that is, the incarnation of the other's own bodily sense, in some ways be comparable to what Derrida calls in this earlier text "endocryptic identification," and in the later text on Nancy, *corpus mysticum*?

At least, this is how I would begin to de-cipher Derrida's own reading at this point, especially concerning the afore-mentioned limit that first appears in the passage of Husserl concerning a sense of incarnation that "will never be mine," that, according to Derrida, Nancy both "touches" and "trans-gresses" as well (meaning also, *with* Merleau-Ponty). In other words, Derrida argues, Nancy's attempt to think this limit as the "simultaneity of distance and contact" is "with" (*avec*) the thinking of Merleau-Ponty who, we remember, was accused of a certain infidelity to Husserl's text, that is, of betraying the idea of "pure phenomenology." What lies beyond this limit of introjection, like Eros contemplating Psyche in her coffin, can only be figured by something akin to an "imaginary and occult" quality of apperception, namely, by an obscure form of self-perception that would approximate mysticism. By this word we are referred back by Derrida to the last citation of Freud, on his deathbed, with which Derrida begins his mediation on Nancy's *Corpus*: "Mysticism is the obscure self-perception of the realm outside the Ego, of the Id [*Mystik die dunkle Selbswhahrnehmung des Reiches ausserhalb des Iches, des Es*]."[21] Earlier I already called attention to the significance of the fact that Derrida begins his entire mediation on "the body (*corpus*) of Jean-Luc Nancy" specifically with a reference to the living corpse of Psyche who is sealed in her coffin. But it is this mysterious body that already pre-figures the sense of another *corpus mysticum* that appears in the absolute sense of what Nancy calls "*The* body" as "the auto-symbolization of an absolute organ ... that exhausts all signification."[22] Moreover, the capitalization of "*The* body" (*Le* corps) refers to an exceptional and singular sense meaning "this body" and "only this body," either figuring the body of Psyche herself, or perhaps more generally echoing the other's bodily

96

sense that remains "without introjection," which becomes in Nancy's phrase, "*The* body" ... "that exhausts all signification." But we might immediately ask whether these two different bodies that will remain "without introjection" share the same sense. Can the other person's singular and un-sharable sense of embodiment (referring to "this other's body" and "only to that singular body" in the appresentation of the other person) become, as it appears in Nancy's text, "*The* body" ... "that exhausts all signification," referring in this case to a pre-originary and ontological structure of ex-appropriation that determines "the other in general" (Nancy)?

If I were to risk a simple (yet perhaps scandalous) anthropological observation, it would be to point out that, in its most "primitive" signification, the Christian religion is also founded upon an exception – perhaps even constituting the universal exception! – to the processes of so-called "normal mourning." From a psychoanalytic point of view, which would originally be associated with Freud, this could certainly be understood as a shared and collective refusal of mourning and the demands for libidinal reorganization that the death of a member of a community normatively commands. (This is most evident in the ritualized and primitive significance enacted by the Christian Eucharist, what is called "the feast of incorporation".) In what I have already identified as a fantastic solution, it has replaced the process of "normal mourning" with a "magical operation" that surpasses this limit and, at the same time, keeps the integrity of the other's living body intact, albeit encrypted within the self. Second, the Christian religion has enfranchised the absolute limit of death by creating a "fetish" of "the body of Christ," that is to say, this one exceptional body, this body which belongs to no other and cannot, therefore, be confused with the body in its simple biological determination, or with "the fleshly comportment" of the body as such. Both of these senses return us to the original event from which this religious signification of the Christian body was born into the world (i.e., the empty tomb, the missing body of Christ, or *Deus Abscondus*), but also to the earliest ritual practices that enact this event precisely through the magical act of incorporation: the eating of the living body of the Christ (the Host), the shared division and distribution (*partage*) by the members of the Christian community of the missing pieces of the body of *Deus Abscondus*. If this primitive signification would appear to border on a collective psychosis, I would immediately refute this simply by stating that there can be no universal psychosis. The meaning of psychosis can only appear as the refusal of a Symbolic (universal) order of significations, and for this reason it would be meaningless to say that there is a universal psychosis. Such an order, if it were to exist, would belong to the Symbolic, which is why the "set of all introjections" that determines the reality of the Christian psyche does not, in the final analysis, belong to the order of the Imaginary (i.e., the Christ-event is not simply a group fantasy).

Second, in what is perhaps the most essential passage of *Corpus*, where he identifies "The body" as the "auto-symbolization of the absolute organ," Nancy writes: "God, Death, Flesh – the triple name of the body in all onto-theology where all signification is exhausted."[23] Elsewhere, he defines the body as the "archi-tectonic of sense," meaning that the specifically Christian body is *omphalos,* the navel, representing the exact place of origin, the creation of world, which is given in the sense of "birthing-toward" or the very exposure to existence: "it is exposing/exposed: *augedehnt*, extension of the effraction that is existence."[24] Of course, this signification of the *omphalos* is present in every religion, in every creation story or myth, as the archi-tectonic topos of the creation of the world that belongs to that religion and refers to a place that is held to be sacred. In Christianity, however, the *omphalos* does not refer to a particular sacred location or holy site that could be memorialized, but to the living topos of the body itself. In other words, the Christian body is a thoroughly mobile archi-tectonic: a mobile Mecca or Jerusalem, Sinai or Olympus, a walking volcano, or Machu Pichu, a wandering Himalayas. The specifically Christian or onto-theologically determined body is the site of creation encrypted *inter feces et urinam* – the site of birth, death, but moreover the site of incarnation where the sense of this world that is bound up the body's own corporeality is exposed to its own singular limit, which is death, and thus is re-born to a new sense, a new creation, a new *Körper-body* (human world).

In order to respond to these questions we must return to Nancy's *Being Singular Plural*, where the very sense of ex-appropriation is schematized as a certain "syncopation" (*syncope*) that occurs in the appresentation of the other person. Here, the technical meaning of syncopation is defined as a temporary displacement of the regular metrical accent, causing the emphasis to shift from a strong to a weak accent. As in music or poetry, it constitutes a disruption of an expected or regular pattern, causing an unexpected or irregular pattern to emerge. This can be understood as the unique method that Nancy devises to render the co-incidence or co-presence of the self and the other precisely by placing emphasis on the "weak accent" (on the "off beat") that will cause the relation of self and other, and other to the self, to become non-synchronous, varied and varying, that is to say, in the form of a syncopated pattern that replaces the regular and measured pattern given by a strong emphasis on "the self," "the subject" or the "Consciousness" in previous metaphysical and phenomenological traditions. In fact, I would argue that all of Nancy's major concepts – *desoeuvrement*, *partager* and *syncope* – are technically derived from this same emphasis on a "weak accent" producing a field of co-presence and co-community that is exactly a syncopated form of singularities. The place of the weak accent in Nancy's schema would be precisely the topic of the other's body, "without introjection," an impossible experience that Consciousness can never give to itself and which remains forever ex-appropriated. As Nancy writes, "It appears inaccessible 'to me' because it is withdrawn from the 'self' in general, and because it is self-outside-itself: it is the other in general, the other that has its moment of identity in the divine Other, which is also the moment of the identity of everything, of universal *corpus mysticum*.'[25] Here again, we must return to Derrida's earlier caution concerning precisely this theme of ex-appropriation that could too easily reproduce the same "intuitionism" by an emphasis on its exact opposite: non-coincidence, non-contemporaneousness and/or alterity. In other words, would this technique of producing, in place of a humanist tradition of intuitionism, a counter-intuitive moment of *ek-stasis*, itself assume the form of an incorporation of the other's alterity, even though this alterity was represented only by the irregular, the uneven, the non-metrical, in other words, in the syncopated form of a "weak intuitionism" (leading perhaps to a "weak humanism," a "weak theology" or even a "deconstructive Christianism" [*sic*])? As in the case of any technique (or *techne*), such a knowledge could easily become too technical or purely formal in the sense of immediately giving itself the power of producing the sense of the "other in general," even by means of an irregular and off-beat pattern. In other words, just as in music, a syncopated and unexpected pattern sooner or later becomes simply another regular pattern, as in the case of Reggae. Consequently, it is not by accident that there is a certain "off beat" or a syncopated measure of *ex-scription* that one comes to find, and even expects to find, in the philosophy of Jean-Luc Nancy. In fact, I would even go so far as to say that Nancy has recently abandoned the phenomenological method in favor of a measure that belongs to the arts, specifically to musical incantation and hymn.[26]

In his commentary on *Being Singular Plural*, Derrida also carefully weighs and ponders this syncopated pattern of appresentation according to its musical analogy, as well as what it claims to measure or to grasp: in a word, the immeasurable.

> It is always the law of parting and sharing at the heart of touching and contact, presentation, appearance, and co-appearance: sharing out as participation and partition, as continuity and interruption, as syncopated beat … At the moment when Nancy's thinking is thus decided (and, as has been noted, it often is), it always sets off to think while measuring exactly the "incommensurable" and measuring itself to the "incommensurable."[27]

Implicitly, Derrida asks how it is possible that Jean-Luc Nancy is able to *exactly* apprehend – albeit in a purely formal or schematic manner – what is precisely incommensurable, that is, inaccessible to any direct intuition, and more importantly, to any means or technique of indirect appresentation. Nancy's thinking is thus decided … setting out to think while measuring *exactly* "the incommensurable." In other words, how can Nancy claim to be so certain about this "*exactly*" in the sense that it becomes a regular measure or meter in the appresentation of self "with" (*avec*) the other? The "incommensurable" would thus correspond to the syncopated measure of Nancy's schema of distance in proximity, the metrics of touching, which is why his thinking around this point (i.e., "*The* body") often appears more like poetry than philosophy. Here, we might immediately observe an allusion to the "path of thinking" recalled in the earlier passage by Derrida concerning those "who have already entered it," particularly in the phrase "it [Nancy's thinking] always sets off to think while measuring exactly...." Derrida's repeated use of the term "exactly" refers to the certainty of the *de-cision*, as well as to his *faith* in the created "measure" around this point; however, it also refers to the identity of "the other that has its moment of identity in the divine Other, which is also the moment of the identity of everything, of *universal corpus mysticum*."[28] As in the earlier passage cited from *Corpus*, Nancy's famous trinity – God, Death, Flesh – is co-implicated in the auto-symbolization of "*The* body" as an absolute organ that "exhausts all signification." However, could "*The* body" here also be defined by means of this logic of incorporation as a pure "spacing" (*espacement, partage*) encrypted within the self? It would then represent the absolute limit placed within the self, but nevertheless outside all possible introjection (a pure *topos*, or a "*parturition without comparition*"), created to save, to keep safe, the other *as* other, as if permanently emptied of all significations – and perhaps in order to "comprehend nothing in it." In this case, "*The* body" would correspond to a cipher in the text of Jean-Luc Nancy, that is, to a cryptonymic production of an "artificial unconsciousness." Again, the "unconsciousness" that concerns any cryptographic reading is not immediately the dynamic unconscious, at least not directly, but rather a purely fabricated or false unconsciousness produced by the technique of a ciphered language or implicit code. How

can one understand "The body ... as auto-symbolization..."
encrypting the signifiers of "God," "Death," and "Flesh" except
as the indication of a ciphered system, or secret *kerygma*? Of
course, this would only be my *thesis*, in the sense of being what I
am de-ciphering in reading what is implicated in Derrida's own
cryptic reading of Jean-Luc Nancy's *Corpus*.

Returning now to my reading of what is already implicit in
this body, immediately following his commentary on the theme
of ex-appropriation in the writings of Nancy, particularly in
reference to *Being Singular Plural*, Derrida immediately links this
explicitly to the subject of "pre-originary mourning," that is, to
the logic of cryptonomy:

> If I have often spoken of pre-originary mourning on this
> subject, and tied that to the motif of ex-appropriation, it has
> been in order to mark that interiorization, in this mourning
> before death, and even introjection, which we often take for
> granted in normal mourning, cannot and must not be achieved.
> Mourning as im-possible mourning – and moreover a-human,
> more than human, pre-human, different from the human "in"
> the human of humanualism.[29]

What is "pre-originary mourning" and what does it have to
do with this subject? The subject, again, is Husserl's passage
concerning whether there can be any substitution possible in the
appresentation of this original ex-appropriation. Immediately
preceding this passage, Derrida writes: "No substitution is
possible!"[30] Surprisingly, however, such a substitution is already
presupposed even in the most fervent claims to preserve (to save,
to be capable of saving) the "unique and other ones" – "*Being
singular plural*, Nancy might say at this point."[31] Here, such a
claim is tantamount to a pre-originary "successful mourning,"

to the mark of an a priori interiorization of what is unique in the other, the trace of an incorporation of the other as other that is even prior to death or to introjection. As Derrida says, the processes of so-called "normal mourning" always already presuppose that mourning is possible on the basis of some "pre-originary mourning" that has been successfully accomplished. Recalling a similar problematic that appeared around the solution of cryptic incorporation – that is, a certain demand for the reality of the loss and of the possibility that is pre-supposed by normal mourning to be capable of internalizing this loss, "which would re-appropriate the alter-ego within My Ego's own properness" – Derrida never seems to stop equivocating or vacillating between the two senses of introjection and incorporation, successful mourning and impossible mourning. Perhaps he is weighing and pondering here exactly which sense is most "proper"? In other words, perhaps cryptic incorporation and its resistance to what normal mourning already presupposes is the best way to preserve the "other *as other*." He raises this question in the earlier text we have been citing, where he points toward an "irreducible ambiguity":

> The question of course could be raised as to whether or not "normal mourning" preserves the object *as other* (a living person dead) inside me. This question – of general appropriation and safekeeping of the other *as other* – can always be raised as the deciding factor, but does it not at the very same time blur the very line it draws between introjection and incorporation, through an essential and irreducible ambiguity?[32]

Concerning this difference, in this earlier text Derrida prefers to leave it undecidable, although in *Le Toucher* he pretends to decide – *with* Husserl and "against" a *certain* Merleau-Ponty (who, as we have seen, implicates Jean-Luc Nancy as well, that is, "too"). As far as a Christian thinking of the flesh is concerned, we have already seen Derrida's earlier critical remark that this thinking is too precipitous in its own decision, too easily decides this question, and perhaps is already decided in advance – especially for those who have already entered this path. (I can only imagine he is not only referring to Christians here, whether or not this Christianity is explicitly avowed or only a secular and cultural pre-condition of philosophical language, but more to those who "believe," to the believers, "the faithful".) Again, however, we must come back to Derrida's implicit claim, which I would argue echoes the earlier claims made by Heidegger around the existential comportment of "faith" (*pistis*). Why would a "Christian philosophy" – although, certainly, the Heidegger of 1927 would never accept such an animal, considering it a "squared circle" – be too precipitous in deciding this question that occurs precisely around the phenomenological limit of introjection itself – ultimately concerning a certain manner (or "technique") of saving-preserving the other *as other*? Could this *ultimately* have something to do, as in the above passage, with the suspicion of an already "presupposed" pre-originary mourning?

In response to these questions, Heidegger's earlier description of the existential comportment of faith may be useful in clarifying what Derrida is pointing to here, specifically with regard to "a Christian thinking of the flesh," if only to "weigh" and "ponder" its thinking. *To have faith means to be able to ontically overcome a pre-Christian existential comportment*; accordingly, "one's pre-Christian *Dasein* [I would prefer to use Derrida's word, *Psyche*, the proper name of the Greek, that is, pre-Christian, Aristotelian "soul" that he first discovers to be encrypted, "in her coffin" in Nancy's *Corpus*] is existentially, ontologically included within faithful existence," which is preserved or "saved" (*aufgehoben*) in a certain way. "Sublated (*aufgehoben*) does not mean done way with, but raised up, kept, and preserved in a new creation."[33] In *Dis-enclosure: The Deconstruction of Christianity*, Nancy also employs Hegel's word, attempting to breathe new life into a concept that has received such bad press: "Let us add we do not even yet know, perhaps, what Hegelian dialectical sublation really is, that perhaps we don't know what negativity is. To find out we must plunge into its heart – a heart that risks being, if I dare say so, Christian."[34] For Heidegger, of course, the pre-Christian content is merely sublated, "preserved," but in such a way that theological thinking is powerless to determine this content ontologically. Certainly, this betrays a prejudice that the existential content of a concept is always pre-Christian (i.e., Greek), which is equal to the ontological determination of the concept's true sense. For example, the Christian concepts of sin and guilt can never "grasp" the existential and ontological contents even though they have "encrypted" this content in an ontic form in the concepts of "guilt" and "sin" themselves. However, if this is a fundamental prejudice in Heidegger's thinking, which I will turn to discuss in the next statement, then it is a prejudice that is constitutive of phenomenology as "the science of Being."

Therefore, what Heidegger is describing by the term *aufgehoben*, a term already made famous by Hegel, is what Derrida has called "encryptment," by which a certain content is incorporated in order that it might be preserved precisely as other (even as the artifact of an earlier existence). "Accordingly, the proper *existentiall* meaning of faith is: faith = rebirth."[35] In other words, a Christian existence defined by "faith = rebirth" will always concern the proper destination of a pre-Christian *psyche*, to again employ Derrida's proper name for it (or her?), but in a manner that simulates a successful mourning. In the occurrence of rebirth, the pre-Christian psyche is estranged by death, but nevertheless remains encrypted within the Christian psyche as "another self" that must be properly mourned, that is, preserved *as an other* who belongs properly to the past of the Christian self. However, it is discovered that this other included in the Christian psyche as another psyche *also* has a body which is defined by its own fleshly comportment; although the psyche is dead (in the past), this body continues to feel and sense according to its own flesh (in the present), becoming a "strange body" that inhabits the Christian psyche, sometimes overcoming it through sin and especially sexuality (*pornea*). It is for this reason that the most intense struggles will occur around the success or the failure of the sublation of this other (dead) psyche in my living psyche, this other strange body in my own proper body, leading to all the problems that have surrounded the Christian determination of the body in historical Christian societies, including our own, especially concerning the proper relation to one's own body and to the bodies of others (and to the bodies of women, especially). In the writings of Origen, for example, the pre-Christian body is compared to the "after-birth," or placenta, the discharge that follows the birth of the living body – one might even call it the dead *khora*. However, this image does not correspond to the dialectic between the Christian psyche and the pre-Christian corpus that I have been describing above. Given the resonance that already exists between "successful sublation" and "successful mourning" in Derrida's earlier text, it is easy to understand why he might allude to the "irreducible" problems of failed intro- jection and impossible mourning, that is, to incorporation or encryptment *"in the thinking of the Christian flesh, tacitly, the caress, in a word, the Christian body.*" What this concerns is a certain "con-fusion" of this strange flesh in the Christian body with the living body of the other person, that is, the other's own existential carnality. The problem occurs when we see that while the pre-Christian psyche is included as other (as a former or dead self that is properly mourned), the pre-Christian flesh, the body of the former self that becomes estranged by rebirth, must henceforth be completely converted and sublated by the living and reborn Christian flesh – as Paul writes, it must be "consumed by everlasting life": "These earthly bodies make us groan and sigh, but we wouldn't like to think of dying and having no body at all. We want to slip into our new bodies so that these dying bodies will, as it were, be consumed by everlasting life" (2 Cor. 5:4). In the opening pages of *Le Toucher*, Derrida perhaps alludes to this flame in describing the fate of Psyche herself in the gruesome image of her body "turned to toast": "(*tostus* means burned, and toasted, from *torreo*, consumed by fire, or incinerated – in a blazing immediacy that pulls out all the stops; and that is why *one has arrived all too soon* [i.e., too quickly, "with quasi-infinite speed"], in a present not yet present but no longer future)...."[36]

On the weight of the above citations, and what they seem to imply (and then only by implication), I will conclude my own reading of the earlier passage concerning the path from an implicit philosophical anthropomorphism to an explicit (if not overt) "Christian thinking of the flesh," in other words, a "Christian phenomenology." Perhaps then the Christian body is precisely a path that leads too easily from one to the other, as if con-fusing the implicit sense of the other's body as that which will forever remain "outside introjection" with the "revealed" sense of the incarnation *of this strange body* (*Körper*) *in the human flesh* (*Leib*). In what manner is this sense "revealed"? Here again, I am only reading Derrida's allusion to the "faithful," those who have already been predisposed to follow a certain path that leads directly from simple phenomenological intuitionism to the Christian body. In what way are they so predisposed? Simply put, by a form of existence that is only revealed in their faith in the *Körper*-body, that is, in the sense of the human world. As Derrida has explicitly remarked elsewhere, the phenomenological concept of the "flesh" (*Fleisch*) already presupposes the human.[37] Can there be any other flesh (*Fleisch*) than the human flesh (*Leib*)? Certainly, one can say "the flesh of the animal," but this already pre-destines the animal to belong to a system of anthropological significations that determines its meaning in relation to the human body, a relation that could even be appropriate or inappropriate in the sense of not eating the flesh (*Fleisch*) of this or that particular animal, of not "touching the flesh of an animal" and of "sacred animals" in particular. One would need to understand the anthropological significations that determine the meaning of the "Christian body" in this regard; and here, I am merely pointing out the strange echo of this anthropological distinction of the human flesh (*Leib*) in the sense accorded to the other's carnal corporeality (*Leiblichkeit*), which must remain "without introjection." And yet, what remains "without introjection" could either be understood as pointing to a body that exists "beyond the limit of introjection," that is, the body I have been attempting to think according to the logic of incorporation, as an encrypted body; or, this body could be understood as "*The* body" that exists beyond in the sense of exhausting every attempt at introjection by means of direct apprehension or strong analogy. But then, this "*The* body" would be "beyond phenomenology" also, since it could never be thought according to the phenomenological method and for this reason it would be fated to remain, strictly speaking, "unthinkable." By contrast, the phenomenological sense of what remains "without introjection" in appresentation of the other person's carnality was, for Husserl, simply the impossibility of two *heres* directly present in the Consciousness of the self-same ego. It would be stating the obvious to say that there is no hint, not even the least trace, of a "divine Other" in this simple limit of introjection, which is useful in allowing me not to confuse my right hand for the other's left, or the other's left hand for my right. As we have seen above in the case of Nancy – and this would be true of Levinas as well, in a different sense – this simple phenomenological truth is "converted" into becoming the source of *a divine mystery*, which is identified with the "divine Other." Thus, what is simple "non-coincidence," which in Husserl is compared to the distinction between the left and right hands, becomes the syncopated beating of "*The* body," the alternating presence–absence that exhausts all significations, "the auto-symbolization of an absolute organ." Therefore, we might ask, does *"The body" merely designate the signification of phallus in the Christian thinking of the flesh?*

Maybe I would prefer to leave this last question for another occasion, and therefore will simply conclude by asking whether either understanding of "the Christian body" would also mark the return of a metaphysical determination of the "essence" of the human. Given that the universality of an essence in this case is not determined by reason, but rather by "*The* body," then the fundamental determination of the essence of the human can never be completely exposed or illuminated by Science, including phenomenology as "the Science of Being." That which cannot be directly apprehended or grasped by any "Science," therefore,

110

can only be grasped either by faith, or indirectly (that is, barely touched) by an obscure form of self-perception approximating mystical incantation (prayer) or poetry (which also, according to Heidegger, is essentially song, *Gesang*). Moreover, any discourse that attempts to "name" (either directly or indirectly), that is, to call forth into presence in order to give a *sense* to, the essence of the human is essentially a "Humanism," and as a result, here I will recall Heidegger's statement that "every humanism is either grounded in a metaphysics or is itself made to be the ground of one."[38] If this is indeed the case, then we might be led to speculate that the earlier historical and philosophical humanisms (*homo romanus*, *renascentia romanticus*, and *studium humanitas*, as well as the humanisms of Marxism and Existentialism), have only recently been surpassed and exceeded by the arrival of a new humanism, or at least by *the Christian revival of an already implicit philosophical anthropocentricism.*

The most remarkable characteristic of this new humanism, as compared with all the earlier ones, is that it would be the weakest of all humanisms in the sense that it does not explicitly name the essence of the *humanitas*, but prefers to leave this essence indeterminate, obscure, mysterious; in essence it "leaves it open" – in the sense of permanently suspended in hospitality – a place for the other, the stranger's body, and the orphaned consciousness.[39] But then this very weakness quickly becomes its greatest strength, since it is through this empty space that it will claim to exhaust, that is, to "disassemble," even to "deconstruct," all the earlier humanisms that *presupposed* the universal essence of the human being to be obvious. But how can this essence be obvious if it is to remain shrouded in a mystery – *that is, unless the sense of the mystery itself should become too obvious?* As for me, concerning this presupposed weakness, as I stated in the beginning concerning the presupposition of a "theological turn," I prefer to remain skeptical (critical, vigilant, even "on guard"). *After all, this same weakness may only be a wolf in sheep's clothing.* Here, I believe I am *with* Derrida in this respect, when he wrote: "Husserl's cautious approach should always remain *before us* as a model of vigilance."[40] In this respect also, I believe I am *with* Dominique Janicaud, who was engaged in a similar debate on French soil, well before it was globalized (or, according to Derrida's coinage, "globalatinized"), and seemed to draw some of the same conclusions concerning what he called the "theological swerve."[41] Therefore, in acknowledgement of Janicaud's earlier efforts and in a gesture intended to keep the question open (before it is closed too precipitously by those who appear to be already decided), I will close my own reading of this later return statement with the same citation of E. M. Cioran from Janicaud's *La Tournant theologique de la phenomenologie francaise* (1991):

> For the unbeliever, infatuated with waste and dispersion, there is no spectacle more disturbing than these ruminants on the absolute … Where do they find such pertinacity in the unverifiable, so much attention in the vague, and so many ardors to seize it?[42]

Notes

A previous version of this statement appeared as "Decrypting 'the Christian Thinking of the Flesh, tacitly, the Caress, in a word, the Christian Body' in *Le Toucher*," *Sophia* 47:3 (2008), pp. 293–310, special issue edited by Jack Reynolds.

1   See Kuhn, *The Structure of Scientific Revolutions.*

2 Nancy, *Dis-enclosure: The Deconstruction of Christianity*, pp. 139–57.

3 Heidegger, *Pathmarks*, p. 53.

4 Derrida, *On Touching: Jean-Luc Nancy*, p. 78.

5 Ibid.

6 Ibid., p. 93.

7 Ibid., p. 110 (emphasis mine).

8 Ibid., p. 93.

9 Ibid., p. 243 (emphasis mine).

10 Ibid., p. 183. Nevertheless, Derrida does not seem to be implying that this other tradition, which is also shared by Didier Franck and others, would be the true inheritor of Husserlian "pure phenomenology," which would be, according to Derrida, "strictly Cartesian," even "more Cartesian than Descartes himself."

11 Ibid., pp. 190–1.

12 Ibid., p. 191.

13 Ibid., pp. 12ff.

14 Ibid., p. 224 (translation modified by Michael Naas in correspondence with the author).

15 Here, I would like to acknowledge the influence of Avital Ronell, who first instructed me in the method of cryptonomy in a graduate seminar conducted at the University of California, Berkeley, in the fall of 1986, the same year that I also attended the seminar conducted by Jean-Luc Nancy. It was also in 1986 that the translated volume of *The Wolf Man's Magic Word: A Cryptonomy* appeared from the University of Minnesota Press, although a translated version of Derrida's foreword to this edition, "Fors," had previously appeared much earlier in a 1977 issue of the *Georgia Review*.

16 See "Incorporation," in Laplanche and Pontalis, *The Language of Psychoanalysis*, pp. 211–12.

17 Derrida, "Fors," p. xvi.

18 Ibid., pp. xvi–xvii (emphasis in original).

19 Ibid., p. xix (emphasis in original, translation modified).

20 Ibid., pp. xvii–xviii.

21 Derrida, *On Touching: Jean-Luc Nancy*, p. 12.

22 Nancy, *Corpus*, p. 66.

23 Ibid.

24 Nancy, *Being Singular Plural*, p. 24.

25 Nancy, *Corpus*, p. 79.

26 The relationship between Nancy's own form of ex-scription and Heidegger's later turn to poetry, and to the poetry of Hölderlin particularly,

bears closer scrutiny, which I cannot perform here. On this subject, see the 1964 letter attached to "Phenomenology and Theology" in the edition of the *Gesamtausgabe*, where Heidegger writes: "Poetic saying [song, *Gesang*] is being in the presence of … and for the god" (Heidegger, *Pathmarks*, p. 61).

27 Derrida, *On Touching: Jean-Luc Nancy*, p. 225.

28 Nancy, *Being Singular Plural*, p. 79. It also bears mentioning that the quoted subtitle of the first tangent in *Le Toucher*, where we find Psyche extended in her coffin, reads "Around her, with such exact and cruel knowledge" (Derrida, *On Touching: Jean-Luc Nancy*, p. ii).

29 Derrida, *On Touching: Jean-Luc Nancy*, p. 192.

30 Ibid.

31 Ibid.

32 Derrida, "Fors," p. xvii.

33 Heidegger, *Pathmarks*, p. 51.

34 Nancy, *Dis-enclosure: The Deconstruction of Christianity*, p. 143.

35 Heidegger, *Pathmarks*, p. 44.

36 Derrida, *On Touching: Jean-Luc Nancy*, pp. 13–14.

37 Ibid., p. 242.

38 Heidegger, *Pathmarks*, p. 245.

39 On this point, I refer the reader to the passage from *Corpus* titled "Étranges corps étrangers" (pp. 9–11).

40 Derrida, *On Touching: Jean-Luc Nancy*, p. 191.

41 I will return again later on to discuss the term "globalatinization," which appears in Derrida's 1994 address, "Faith and Knowledge," particularly in a series of "cryptic notes" on the meaning of the Latin term *religio*. In fact, as I will argue below, Derrida appears to agree with Heidegger that the "'return of religious' would signify nothing but the persistence of a Roman determination of religion (*religio*)," a determination that is premised upon "the dominant juridical system and the concept of the State" (Derrida and Vattimo, *Religion*, p. 72).

42 Quoted by Janicaud, *Phenomenology and the "Theological Turn,"* p. 69.

5

Philosophical Fundamentalism Today

Let's now return to discuss in more detail the proposition already invoked in the previous statement, which is taken from Heidegger's 1927–28 lecture course in Marburg: "*theology is a positive science, and as such, therefore, is absolutely different from philosophy*."[1] Here, Heidegger's precise use of the term "absolute" refers to a difference that is not soluble, that cannot be mixed up, diluted, or watered down. It is for this reason, as he states later on, that there can be no "Christian philosophy." Why? Because philosophy "demands a fundamental shift of view and this immediately sets it on a divergent path from any theological viewpoint." In fact, according to Heidegger's dictum, such a divergence cannot even be called a "shared conviction," in the sense of Nancy's *partager* (both to share and to divide up, or to partition), since it always appears that it is philosophy that departs from theology by means of its own scientific method, which in this case is the phenomenological method properly speaking. Consequently, as opposing sciences, philosophy and theology cannot share (much less divide up) the same region of being and of beings that belong to them. It is because they belong to absolutely different regions that they have different points of view, which also suggests that the difference we are speaking of here is not merely conceptual or linguistic, as if theology would disclose the same region of being by another name (or "language game").

If this "absolute difference" were not stated clearly enough, a little further on, in a famous passage, Heidegger recasts this ontico-ontological opposition in much stronger terms as an "existential opposition": "This peculiar relationship does not exclude but includes the fact that *faith*, as a specific possibility of existence, is in its innermost core the mortal enemy of the *form of existence* that is an essential part of *philosophy* and that is factically ever-changing."[2] In a sense, one could call Heidegger at this stage a "fundamentalist philosopher," in the same sense as we say fundamentalist Christian or Muslim. In the above passage, the three terms that are italicized are *faith*, *form of existence* and *philosophy*; this underlines and clarifies the extreme nature of the opposition. Philosophy is not opposed to theology, but rather to faith as a *form of existence*. Faithful existence is the "mortal enemy" of philosophical existence almost in the same sense that it has often been said by some today that Islam is the mortal enemy of Christianity. What is peculiar about this absolute opposition between world-views is that philosophy, for its part, does not even want to encounter this mortal enemy in violent combat. As I said above, it is for this reason that it is philosophy that seems to withdraw from this potentially lethal struggle and exist in an entirely different world; it is only in this manner that mortal enemies can live in relative peace. Moreover, it is only by understanding the opposition as one between absolutely "incompossible worlds," according to a Leibnizian schema, that philosophy and theology can ever hope to "communicate" with one another, or belong to a "community of the sciences" free from any "illusions and weak attempts at mediation." Therefore, it is only from the standpoint of an absolute difference, without possible mediation, that philosophy and theology can ever hope to engage in a "genuine dialogue." Absolute difference is beyond conflict or strife, and separation is itself a form of peaceful co-existence between mortal enemies; there is even the possibility of communication, but only under the precondition that this difference is affirmed by each party as absolute, not subject to any attempt to turn it into a form of relative difference (such as the difference between two cultures, or between two ideological points of view). For Heidegger, it would seem that in the affirmation of an absolute difference overt expressions of conflict or struggle (*Kampf*) are suspended, but only assuming that actual violence or overt combat could break out again if the sense of this difference is weakened in any way. What is interesting to me in all this is the manner in which Heidegger, in 1928, and in a way that almost resembles the "friend-enemy" distinction of Schmidt, is attempting to conceive of the difference between philosophy and theology on the model of a "strong difference" of political theology. It is only on the basis of a permanent condition of absolute war that these entities can co-exist, even though this co-existence is divided into incompossible worlds, and their forms of existence can only exist peacefully in their completely separate spheres.

In order to further explicate this extreme opposition – if not antagonism – we would also need to return to Heidegger's earlier lecture course during the Winter of 1920–21 on *The Phenomenology of Religious Life*.[3] Briefly, I will highlight the use of the term "factically" here with regard to the "forms of existence" that are said to belong to philosophy and faith. In the earlier lecture, factically refers to the manner in which *Dasein* stands out from factical life existence (*Lebensdasein*, perhaps closely approximating what Agamben calls "bare life"), but also from the historical context, understood as the inherited meaning of past cultures. In turning against "mere factical existence" (or bare naked life) consciousness also turns "against history"; or, phrased affirmatively, *Dasein* demands its own history that emerges from out of its own factical existence. As Heidegger writes, "it wants to be a new creation, be it an entirely original one, a 'great synthesis,' 'away from the barbaric,' or however one names these tendencies."[4] We can clearly see how this impulse can refer to a specifically (or as Heidegger says "primitive") Christian form of existence, particularly under its Pauline determination, where the above antagonism is set into the historical meanings of conversion and proclamation, as a differentiation between the converted Christian self and the pre-Christian self, on the one hand, and the non-Christian or worldly-self (including the pagan), on the other. But let us keep in mind here that the turn toward the historical as the region where *Dasein's* factical existence will emerge is, in fact, a turning away from the meaning of mere factical life existence (*Lebensdasein*), which *Dasein* finds to be alien, or not to concern its own life but merely the life of the species. However, this reaction to the simple meaning of bare life is then transferred onto the field of the historical itself, as a reaction to the strange and alien life of an other, "a barbaric way of life," projected onto the *Lebensdasein* that belongs to past cultures now determined to be alien, which also prepares the way for projecting the "lifeworld" of alien cultures into the past. In its primordial religious determination, faith is certainly a reaction against bare life even when the latter becomes the expression of theology; thus, the disclosure of existence by faith is always distinguished from the disclosure of being determined by the fact of merely living. The existence of a God or divine source of life is essentially involved in this turning away from the naked sense of life, which again must be understood as reactive, even though this reaction is usually concealed by what appears as a positive or affirmative gesture. (I will return in the next statement to this double gesture of affirmation, which hides or conceals a negative moment of rejection, which I will demonstrate by taking up Derrida's reading of the "return of religion" according to what he calls the "gesture of pacification," and under a "double horizon of the Death of God."[5])

For now, simply put, to proclaim faith in something (a God, a divine source of life, an inspiration or the intervention of a spiritual daemon or a metaphysical principle) is always to decide against another factically determined meaning of existence. (According to the Pyrrhonist skeptical doctrine, to deny something is actually to give one's assent to its negation.) Therefore, to have faith is to be, first and foremost, "against." I have been underlining this "against" bare existence or naked life, then, against something else that is defined as "historical." It is for this reason that faith also leads to proclamation, even to self-proclamation (such as in the statements "I am Christian" or "I am Muslim," perhaps even touching the self-proclamation of Yahweh, "I am that I am"), leading to the historical disclosure between different historical traditions of faith, in short, between different religions. One wonders, according to Heidegger's hypothesis, whether the origin of religion is always bound up with this reaction to bare life that, in turn, is displaced onto the historical emergence of differences between cultural forms of existence. For example, we might see this same double movement of reaction and hostility that determines the historical emergence of new social identities, even including sexual or ethnic identities, which are also tied to the creation of new cultures and new proclamations of a factical existence that is shared in common (*Mitsein*), but which at the same time always seem to appear "against" other differences that are ascribed to past cultural and social forms of existence – the differences determined by Eurocentric historical culture or heterosexual social identity, for example. Moreover, these new proclamations of "existential difference" might even be said to resemble positions of faith. Although these new cultures of faith do not always strictly appear in the form of religious phenomena, I would argue that they share the same sense of facticity, born from the same demand for new meaning and the creation of a new living culture, and thus could be said to belong to the same history as the history of religions, which is to say *the struggle of Life against the Historical*. As Heidegger remarks, whether understood in a positive sense bound up with the diversity of historical formations, or in the negative sense in which history appears as a burden or hindrance to the moment of creation, "the historical is disturbing: against it, life seeks to assert and secure itself."[6]

But what does Heidegger mean when he determines the form of existence "that is an essential part of philosophy" is "factically ever-changing"? Implicitly, this names two distinct "attitudes" that Heidegger is ascribing to philosophical existence:

1. That philosophy is a form of existence that is factically, which is to say historically, ever-changing, along with the changing conditions of knowledge (in other words, philosophy is the eidetic expression of changing material conditions, a definition that seems to echo that of Marx, and the later Althusser, concerning the history of philosophy as the expression of different ideological forms of life pertaining to the real relationships that comprise any given society).

2. That the hostility between philosophy and faith emerges historically from the fact that the form of existence of faith belongs to or is likened to another culture that philosophy reacts against in the creation of its own history. To say that this hostility is historical, however, presupposes that other forms of faith could emerge to take the place of theology in other historical moments; thus "absolute difference" could take the form of a reaction against religion in one historical moment, bourgeois morality in the next, and a reaction against "faith in science" or in a techno-scientific reason, in a third moment.

In taking up Heidegger's earlier thesis of the absolute difference between philosophy and theology, however, I would like to maintain (at least provisionally, suspending judgment) its sharp dividing line, *whether or not I factically believe that it exists* (i.e., whether or not I give my assent to its factual negation), if only to cause something like our contemporary historical moment to appear on either side of a line that has been crossed through, if not precipitously crossed out entirely by some philosophers and theorists today. I am saying this in obvious light of the fact that, *contra* Heidegger, not only is there something that could be called "Christian philosophy" or even "Christian decon-structionism," but that many philosophers and theologians today are speaking in ways that are virtually indistinguishable, and are even relying on the same authorities. This is not simply to say that many so-called philosophers are reading the Christian Bible again with a renewed and somewhat peculiar fervor; although this is certainly the case and we could easily list off the names of the most illustrious members of a certain tradition of continental philosophy who are also members of a newly founded Bible study group in philosophy, including Žižek and Badiou. This might even be called, in the colloquial sense, a "religious phenomenon." However, I find it peculiar not only in the sense that this would not have been "thinkable" as recently as twenty years ago in the very same tradition of philosophy – but more so in that this renewed interest in the Christian Bible should come at precisely this moment, historically speaking, and in the context of a geopolitical reality marked by a renewed hostility between what could be called the two major religions of the Book, or of the "Book of books." I wonder: would this phenomenon not signal a weakening of the absolute difference posited earlier by Heidegger? Although Heidegger forecloses the very possibility of Christian philosophy, famously likened to a squared circle, he still seems to allow for occasions when this difference becomes relativistic and weakened by what he calls "illusions and by attempts of weak mediation." However, this still presupposes a fundamental hostility that is merely papered over by pacific and ecumenical feelings. Which raises the most important question: why has the "implicit and presupposed theological turn of phenomenology or philosophy" not resulted in more instances of open hostility or antagonism between these two former sciences, if indeed they can any longer be called sciences today?

Perhaps this would be my first hypothesis (which I cannot take up here, but will return to in the seventh return statement around the return of St. Paul), namely that it has something to do with the decline of an identification with science, and with the fact that neither discourse seems to adhere to the notion of a scientific method as the basis for understanding its truth claims. Moreover, is it still the case that "what is called philosophy" today names a form of existence that is absolutely opposed to faith? If not, how then can we account for its "fundamental shift in point of view," or "modified attitude," that formerly set philosophy on its own divergent path (at least from the modern period onward) *in order to become philosophy in the first place?* Do philosophy and theology share the same region of being, ontically speaking, or belong to the same pre-philosophical disclosure of Being ontologically? Or rather, has this earlier opposition been absolutely sublated (*aufgehoben*), in the sense of being both surpassed/destroyed and preserved in another opposition from which both philosophy and theology derive their shared identity today in the sharing/dividing up of the post-secular? Who then is the "mortal enemy" of a theologico-philosophical or a philosophico-theological form of existence today? Here we might briefly turn to the last text by Deleuze and Guattari, which attempts to answer the question "What is Philosophy?," where we find little mention of the presupposed "absolute difference" with theology as the condition of philosophy. Rather, the absolute difference that appears in this text is with capitalism, and specifically a form of communication that exists in the language of marketing, in conceptual art and advertising.[7] In fact, one can take up Heidegger's own major themes and "pointers" found in the 1964 appendix to *Philosophy and Phenomenology* and find them repeated and rehearsed in Deleuze and Guattari's 1991 text, specifically, "what is thinking?" and "how does philosophy communicate its concepts?," for which Deleuze and Guattari provide the answer – by means of a "creation" that in some sense must be posed "against" an historical past or another cultural point of view.

On the other hand, regarding "what is called theological thinking" today, one might immediately point to the fact that the tradition of modern theology in North America (but also in the

United Kingdom, Germany, and France) is primarily influenced by a certain post-Heideggerian tradition of philosophy, including "deconstruction." Thus, students in many religion departments – I am speaking from first-hand experience, since I have even participated in this "movement" myself – often spend less time reading classical theological sources or the writings of systematic theologians like Aquinas, Barth, Lonergan, or Tillich, than they do reading the same continental philosophers who we found above reading the Christian Bible. In other words, what Heidegger earlier defined as the science of theology referred only to the historical body of that science at the time he was writing in 1929, and thus refers specifically to systematic theology or to practical theology in both the Protestant and Catholic traditions. Although Heidegger would later on, in 1961, take notice of a fundamental transformation in this same tradition of theology that would make his own definitions outdated, in this earlier text he could not have known that his own philosophy would become one of the major influences on this transformation in the manner of "speaking and writing theologically" (that is, as a method of what he earlier defined as "non-objectifying thinking"). In fact, ironically, his own speculative statement that if he were "to write a theology the word Being would be crossed through" has actually been taken up by many theologians, beginning with theologians in Germany early on, such as Rahner and Bultmann, or in France and North America by Gabriel Vahanian, Thomas J.J. Altizer, and Charles Winquist, as a recipe for creating a tradition of "negative theology," or more recently, in the writings of Jean-Luc Marion and John D. Caputo, of a "weak theology."

Today, therefore, not only is something like Christian philosophy possible, it is now said to be the essential form of the renewal of the phenomenological tradition in France, or the destiny of the "deconstructive turn" in North America. Moreover, according to Jean-Luc Nancy, this is because the historical opening of what he calls the "deconstructive operation" announcing or proclaiming (perhaps even in the sense of *evangelion*, "good news") the end of the History of Metaphysics is essentially bound up with the original horizon of Christianity, or the Christian epoch of this history. Thus, the deconstructive announcement of closure proclaims the end of this horizon. According to Nancy, "in it, the end itself is operative and in the proclamation and as the proclamation, because the end that is proclaimed is always an *infinite end*."[8] This is the hidden secret of Christianity that the operation of deconstruction openly reveals as its own secret, even as its "kerygma," as theologians would say. Thus, returning to the above statement, not only can we say there is a Christian philosophy, we can also say (without sarcasm) that *deconstruction is "always already" essentially Christian.* This is Nancy's own hypothesis: that the "gesture of deconstruction" which operates on or proclaims an opening that is "neither simply critical nor perpetuating ... is only possible in Christianity, even though it is not formulated intentionally from within it."[9] Accordingly, we might even speak of an unconscious opening that is unintentionally operated by deconstruction, almost in the sense of a *lapsus calumni*, and perhaps it is for this reason that "the meaning of deconstruction," at least until now, has always remained ambiguous for us. "The Open," as Nancy says (or "the free," as Hölderlin also called it), "is essentially ambiguous" (like "deconstruction" I might add). "It is the entire self-destructive or self-deconstructive ambiguity of Christianity."[10]

At this point, I will return to my major question (or provocation, if you like): "What happened to the absolute difference between philosophy and theology?" If my first hypothesis was that this has something to do with the decline of scientific method in a certain continental tradition of philosophy, and even in the field of phenomenology itself premised on the singular disclosure of "the flesh" (as I have addressed in the last statement concerning Derrida's own observations in *Le Toucher*), then the corollary moment in academic theological discourse would be the marked decline of systematic or practical theology. Therefore, my second hypothesis concerns the aforementioned "sense of ambiguity." What is ambiguity but the expression, whether lexical or semantic, of a "weakened difference"? Thus, the "absolute difference" earlier posited by Heidegger has become an "ambiguous difference" that has led both theological and philosophical regions of knowledge, once they have "foreclosed" their relation to science (whether in its Cartesian determination as "*La Science*" or in terms of Hegelian "Absolute Knowledge"), to confront the most essential ambiguity with regard to the relationship between faith and knowledge. In other words, what would the form of existence called philosophy be without the claim, even if in the form of a pretension, to become "a science of Being"? Likewise, what would theological knowledge become if it did not pretend to systematically study both the origin and meaning of religious phenomena? For example, it is not simply by accident that anthropology has emerged in most religion departments today to take over the former position occupied by the science of theology, which has merely become a manner of "philosophizing otherwise."

As far as the earlier distinction between faith and reason goes, upon which, according to Caputo, the distinction between philosophy and theology supposedly rests, this has merely become the distinction between two different kinds of faith, by which he means the two kinds of "*seeing as*."[11] Here again, we should recall that the original meaning of science was determined as a manner of seeing, which also determines the way in which the world appears according to a scientific point of view; this is why Heidegger later succinctly defined science as "the theory (*theoria, vision*) of reality," which also entails what reality looks like or how it appears *as reality*.[12] In a post-Enlightenment world, however, the vision of reality revealed by modern science has lost all credibility and appears as just another form of faith, or worse, "as Ideology" (Caputo's "seeing as"), which has no more credibility than the pre-scientific theories of reality, namely philosophy and theology, which have returned today to fill the void left by the decline of modern scientific hegemony. This would be my second hypothesis concerning the so-called "theological turn of philosophy today," which in my view has less to do with the return of an earlier theological discourse – since this is certainly not the case as I have commented above! – and more with the return of a pre-scientific (even pre-Cartesian) determination, not of philosophy which is resolutely postmodern in its "language games," *but rather of faith in reason itself.*

Perhaps, echoing Nancy's claim concerning the unintentional lapsus performed by the gesture of deconstruction, in as much as most postmodern philosophies were originally founded upon an anti-Cartesian and counter-modernity (or anti-Enlightenment) gesture, a gesture that has recently been judged by its critics to have exhausted all its resources and been bankrupted by its own earlier anti-humanist sentiments, the return to a pre-Cartesian relationship between knowledge and faith might be seen as one possible way to salvage a sinking ship and extend the postmodern language game for as long as possible. Here, I am simply calling attention to the fact that Caputo himself reduces the distinction between philosophy and theology to a "language game," following Wittgenstein and Lyotard, and the abiding purpose of any language game is to postpone indefinitely the point of its termination. As Caputo writes in *Philosophy and Theology*:

> But the undeniable result of the postmodern turn was to make it possible for religious and theological discourse to assert its rights. Just like the language of art and ethics, religious discourse, too, constitutes its own "form of life," as Wittgenstein would have called it. This means that certain irreducible things get done there, certain things that could only get done by switching into "the language game" of religion, which includes uniquely discursive forms all its own – like prayer, which means not only talking *about* God, but also talking *to* God.[13]

But what of the absolute hostility that was formerly presupposed between faithful existence and philosophical or scientific existence? In most cases, any further separation between "the two cultures" has been dismissed out of hand by the proponents of the theological turn and the new materialism alike as the vestige of an earlier "dogmatic scientific rationalism" – which is reduced to credulity, as another form of faith. (Here, I simply quote the major proclamation by Nancy himself on "the end of this tradition of philosophy": "True, there have been debates on the theme 'Is there or is there not a Christian philosophy?', debates that have sunk in the quagmire to which they were destined by their very formulation."[14]) Moreover, as I already recounted in the introduction, any of the earlier styles of polemical opposition to the belief in a culture of progress, any acerbic suspicion concerning the role of technology, of which Heidegger has been charged, or even any "Voltaire-like" enmity toward "the return of religion," have themselves been accused of philosophical reductionism, "like the cynics of old." In other words, today, just as in the dark age of Enlightenment, it seems that anyone who openly speaks of religion in a critical tone is assuming a personal risk, even though this risk may be purely symbolic in the more secularized regions of the globe. (Of course, in other regions, this is certainly not, or not yet, the case.) Therefore, in view of these dominant judgments, one can only speculate concerning the future of what is called "critical philosophy," which cannot merely be reduced to a style belonging to the historical formation of several discursive formations that have been assembled under the banner of "Critical Theory" (which, today, I would say, is in the process of becoming outmoded as well). For example, in the frequent statements announcing the "end of theory," which interestingly enough began at the exact moment of its emergence, those who have proclaimed themselves to be against a certain tradition of theory (for being too "Eurocentric," "elitist," "linguistically centered," "correlationist," etc.) have performed both an affirmation and a turning away from an even earlier culture in the history of philosophy, in one and the same gesture, but especially in the case of deconstruction which has been judged by many to be too Kantian in its basic sentiments and for its virulent and "hyperbolique" form of negativity. I would even say that what this gesture amounts to is a manner of both repeating and turning away from a certain history of "Critique" to which the history of deconstruction is itself subscribed, and which is evident in the writings of Nancy and Caputo themselves, and thus is one of the subterranean and implicit aspects of their own return statements.

More recently, let us say in the last five years or so, a third return statement has emerged around the theme of "radical atheism" in the work by Martin Hägglund, who seeks to "inherit" the legacy of deconstruction and, at the same time, to "salvage" the possibility of its future (that is, in light of its historical destruction) by means of an operation that can perhaps best be described as an "auto-immunitary logic." Hägglund's entire effort to "systematize" and thus to "fortify his logic," that is, "to reaffirm the legacy in order to cause it to *live on* [to survive] in a different way," amounts to a logic of immunizing those parts of Derrida's own corpus that could threaten the total logic of the system itself – at least, the system that Hägglund discriminates as essential to his own logic of the trace – which is to say, those parts that function against "the standards of a [purely] philosophical logic." And yet, what are those parts of Derrida's body proper that are discovered to function today as anti-bodies that threaten to destroy the immunitary system belonging to the body proper and thus threaten the very survival of the deconstructive legacy that Hägglund wants to salvage, except the very aspects that belong to Derrida's own "inconsistent" and auto-immunitary logic – which is to say, his own inconsistent "politics," his own inconsistent "ethics," his own inconsistent "subjectivity" (or auto-biography), his own inconsistent "desire" to survive *as himself*?[15] Unfortunately, because "like everyone else, Derrida was certainly liable to be inconsistent," Hägglund must discriminate between what he identifies as a "completely different logic altogether," one which is analytically coherent and systematically uniform in all its instances, which can be "measured against the standards of all philosophical logic," and what he identifies as the traces of logical inconsistency that belong to Derrida's own thinking of identity, desire, ethics, and politics.[16] Of course, in his own defense, Hägglund states this intention up front, thus without treachery or perjury, namely, that his own manner of "inheriting" is not to "conserve piously," but rather to inherit in the manner of "critical discrimination," which would amount to the most discriminating selection of certain traces of the work, and at the same time, the auto-suppression and immunization of other traces, in order to best insure the survival of the host. Hence, as he defines his own procedure, "autoimmunity is for me the name of a decon-structive logic that should be measured against the standards of philosophical logic."[17] Finally, this statement of the intention occurs immediately after the declaration to treat Derrida's logic of immunity and auto-immunity according neither to Derrida's own use of these terms, nor in association with their biological meaning, but once again, finally, in accordance with "the standards of philosophical logic."[18]

I realize that the above observations might appear provocative for some, especially as each of these major return statements concerning the legacy of deconstruction all claim to perform their interpretation in the name of a certain fidelity to Derrida himself. Nevertheless, I am not so certain that these works maintain what Derrida calls "fidelity" to his own sense of critique and to his own self-proclaimed gesture of affirmation, "yes, yes" ("*oui, oui*"). Simply put, in reading Derrida one seldom witnesses an affirmation posed on the basis of a previous renunciation (i.e., *non, oui*), particularly when taking up a previous philosopher or historical tradition of philosophy (Cartesianism, for example), which we might view as an act of naïve historicism.[19] As in all things, Derrida's manner of opening the historical past, or of repeating the historical present between its two limits of closure and end (in short, his manner of "historicizing philosophy"), could never be accused of being naïve. Therefore, with this disclaimer, I will end my general remarks on what I have called "philosophical fundamentalism today."

Notes

1 Heidegger, *Pathmarks*, p. 41.

2 Ibid., p. 53.

3 Heidegger, *The Phenomenology of Religious Life*, p. 35.

4 Ibid.

5 Derrida and Vattimo, *Religion*, p. xx.

6 Heidegger, *The Phenomenology of Religious Life*, p. 26.

7 See the conclusion to Deleuze and Guattari's *What is Philosophy?*, pp. 201ff.

8 Nancy, *Dis-enclosure: The Deconstruction of Christianity*, p. 150.

9 Ibid., p. 148.

10 Ibid., p. 157.

11 Caputo, *Philosophy and Theology*, p. 57.

12 Heidegger, *Question Concerning Technology and Other Essays*, pp. 115ff.

13 Caputo, *Philosophy and Theology*, p. 53.

14 Nancy, *Dis-enclosure: The Deconstruction of Christianity*, p. 139.

15 Hägglund, *Radical Atheism*, p. 12. "One question that is bound to arise, then, is whether there are aspects of Derrida's work that do not adhere to the radically atheist logic I develop, especially since it stands in sharp contrast to the readings proposed by many other major interpreters. My response is that even if one is able to find passages in Derrida that cannot be salvaged by the logic of radical atheism, it is far from enough to refute the reading I propose here. *Like everyone else, Derrida was certainly liable to be inconsistent*" (emphasis mine).

16 Ibid. As Hägglund qualifies his method of reading in the conclusion of his introduction: "I not only seek to explicate what Derrida is saying; I seek to develop his arguments, fortify his logic, and pursue its implications. An instructive example is my treatment of the notion of 'survival.' Derrida repeatedly indicates that it is of central importance for his entire oeuvre, but he never provides an explicit account of the logic of survival and its ramifications for our thinking of identity, desire, ethics, and politics."

17 Ibid.

18 Given that the logic of immunity and auto-immunity is so central to the argument, for the reader's benefit, I will quote Derrida's own definition of this logic from "Faith and Knowledge":

> The "immune" (*immunis*) is freed or exempted from the charges, the service, the taxes, the obligations (munus, root of the common

of community). This freedom or this exemption was subsequently transported into the domains of constitutional or international law (parliamentary or diplomatic immunity), but it also belongs to the history of the Christian Church and to canon law; the immunity of temples also involved the inviolability of the asylum that could be found there (Voltaire indignantly attacked this "immunity of temples" as a "revolting example" of "contempt for the laws" and of "ecclesiastical ambition"); Urban VIII created a congregation of ecclesiastical immunity: against taxes and military service, against common justice (privilege designated as that of the *for*) and against police searches, etc. It is especially in the domain of biology that the lexical resources of immunity have developed their authority. The immunitary reaction protects the "indemnity" of the body proper in producing antibodies against foreign antigens. As for the process of auto-immunization, which interests us particularly here, it consists for a living organism, as is well known and in short, of protecting itself against its self-protection by destroying its own immune system. As the phenomenon of these antibodies is extended to a broader zone of pathology and as one resorts increasingly to the positive virtues of immuno-depressants destined to limit the mechanisms of rejection and to facilitate the tolerance of certain organ transplants, we feel ourselves authorized to speak of a sort of general logic of auto-immunization. It seems indispensable to us today for thinking the relations between faith and knowledge, religion and science, as well as the duplicity of sources in general (Derrida, *Acts of Religion*, p. 436n).

19 On the question of naïve historicism, see also Fredric Jameson's reply to Ian Hunter in "How Not to Historicize Theory."

6

Living and Dying Under the Double Horizon of the Death of God

And yet, immediately following the cautionary remarks of the preceding statement, I will also risk attributing a kind of "faith" (*fides*, "fidelity," and not *pistis*, the Christian concept of faith) to Derrida's later reflections on "the return of religion." In fact, Derrida increasingly resorts to this word himself, in the sense of an act of faithful adherence to obligations, duties, responsibilities, vows or promises; at the same time, he also underscores the fact that a common (or naïve) understanding of "strict adherence" is factically impossible, particularly in the case of responsibility, or in vows and promises (see, for example, "*Le perjure*"[1]). In most cases, however, his recourse to the phrase "fidelity to" will concern his "reading" of a certain historical tradition of philosophy, or even the act of fidelity to a particular philosopher. For example, in the third statement I already traced these claims of fidelity to the phenomenological tradition of Husserl, if not in this case the strict observance of Husserl's own phenomenological gesture; thus, I quote again the passage in *Le Toucher*: "Husserl's cautious approach should always remain before us as a model of vigilance."[2]

Of course, in almost all of Derrida's philosophical works, there is a persistent, if not self-tortured, statement of "fidelity" to the work of Heidegger; even in light of the fact that any "strict adherence" to this philosopher's work, much less any faith in this philosopher himself, was strictly impossible, as Derrida openly remarks at many points. Nevertheless, even when it is not openly stated, a certain fidelity is performed through citation and reference, and I would add that this performative citationality seems to increase in his final works, and particularly around the questions of religion, or the divine. In "Faith and Knowledge," not only is there the implication of fidelity to two earlier works "on religion" by Kant and by Bergson, but I also find it interesting that Derrida frequently makes reference to the philosophy of Voltaire alongside his references to Heidegger.[3] In fact, in this text, Voltaire and Heidegger are found to be united in the same tradition in their opposition to the Roman Church, and even in their vehement anti-Christianity, by what Derrida calls "their declared, sometimes nostalgic preference for the same tradition of primitive Christianity"; that is to say, Heidegger and Voltaire are declared as "proto-Catholics."[4]

Secondly, as in all of Derrida's work, the question of fidelity can never take the place or be posed outside of the question of translation. For example, the very act of translation must always presuppose fidelity, even before any question of the translator's moral character or intentionality is even raised. It demands accuracy and precision. (I would even prefer to describe this accuracy in terms of "high fidelity" that is, the degree to which the output of a system accurately *reproduces* the essential characteristics of its input signal.) In fact, Derrida's entire meditation in the text can be understood as addressing problems surrounding fidelity in the act of translating the word "religion." The problems are twofold: Firstly, there is no, let us say, original word for religion (the thing, the phenomenon), according to

Indo-Europeanist Émile Benveniste, only various "equivalents." As an aside, I would point out that one has to pay careful attention anytime there is a mention of Benveniste in Derrida's text. One quickly finds that there is always a frustration of any simplistic etymological impulse to find the origin of a term in question, a frustration that is only underlined by the simplistic belief that origins are pure and the source uncontaminated. Thus, there is a Nietzschean quality to the frustration of this belief, which translates into a Derridean practice of deconstructing a logocentric belief that the word is most closely approximate or present to the thing in its origin. One quickly finds that this is not the case with regard to the word religion, and this is underlined in Derrida's reading of Benveniste's etymological analysis, particularly concerning what he will identify as a certain "logical scandal" in the fact that there is no single etymological source for the thing called "religion" except through its various equivalents that I have already listed earlier – i.e., first, the Greek term *threskeia* (cult, ritual observance); second, the ambiguous senses accorded to the Latin term *religio* (in one sense meaning "to have scruples," in another more "Christian" sense of *religare* meaning "bond or obligation"); finally, adding to Benveniste's original list, we locate a third sense of religion referring to the Holy from the Latin *sacer*, or the German *heilig* (also meaning "whole," "soundness in health," or in Derrida's reading, the overdetermined tension between "immunity" and "auto-immunity").

But what is this, Derrida asks? How can you claim to define the thing when there is, strictly speaking, no clearly demarcated original source for its definition? What are we speaking about when we say, or attempt to think together, "religion"? Even the attempt "to think religion otherwise" would immediately be contradicted by the fact that there was no-thing in the first place, that is, no single meaning or determination that might be differentiated from its new expression, conceptualized differently and even by means of *différance*, thereby subsequently transformed in the determination of its "essence." Here, in this positive discovery, any simple claim to fidelity that might inform the etymological impulse (or return to the source) is confounded by what Derrida calls a "logical scandal." For example, even if one were to claim that the original Latin sense of "*religio*" were adequate as an "original meaning" this is doubly confounded by another scandal that Derrida explicitly calls our attention to – that the contemporary sense of "*religio*" is no longer accurately found to be derived from its Latin root, designating "having scruples," which according to Benveniste had already been mixed up "by the Christians," who invented a new sense of the term from *religare*, meaning "bond or tie." Moreover, today, its so-called "original meaning," which Derrida reminds us it never had (a single meaning, that is), has become up-rooted and now circulates around the globe, and even in outer space in global telecommunication satellites. In fact, "religion" is not even a Latin word today; it is an Anglo-American Latinized hybrid. As Derrida writes: "For everything that touches religion in particular, for everything that speaks 'religion,' for whoever speaks religiously or about religion, Anglo-American remains Latin. *Religion* circulates in the world, one might say, like an *English word <comme un mot anglais>* that has been to Rome and taken a detour to the United States."[5]

Consequently, Derrida cautions us to think these etymological, logical, and geopolitical scandals together, which we might too hastily call the "return of religion." Why hastily? Because, as he goes on to explain, there may have been no "religion" before its return in the first place, that is, there is no *religion* (the word, the thing) before the "return of religion," that is, no "*religio*" before its *globalatinization*. For this reason, "the said 'return of the religious,' which is to say the spread of a complex and overdetermined phenomenon, is not a simple return, for its globality and its figures (tele-techno-media-scientific, capital-istic, politico-economic) remain original and unprecedented."[6] Therefore, not only are we too hasty in talking about "religion" even before we know what it is we are talking about or whether we are maintaining fidelity to a "proper translation" of the thing in question, as to the original meaning of its source, but already in speaking of "the return of religion" we may be betraying any appeal to its source and participating in the very spreading of the gospel of globalatinization. This would result from the simple pretension to "think the meaning of religion," or as the recent theoreticians of religion might say, "to think theologic-ally," without also thinking – at the same time – the global and planetary machines ("tele-techno-media-scientific, capitalist, politico-economic") that are most responsible for producing the meaning of "religion" today. In other words, we are already speaking like Americans who, as we all know – or, as the French say, "*toute le monde*" (everyone knows) – often speak too hastily about things they know too little about, particularly when it comes to other so-called "world religions." Consequently, I would imagine that for most individuals living in other parts of the world, "religion" today would strike them as being more like a foreign word, *comme un mot anglais*, which could be colloqui-ally translated ... "as the Americans say, 'religion'."

What then is "globalatinization," or, specifically, the con-temporary Anglo-American "return of religion"? According to Derrida, this *religio* belongs to an apparatus that first emerges in Rome and takes a detour through the United States, an apparatus of global international law *and* of a global political rhetoric. In taking up the first part of this definition, we would need to ask what is an apparatus? Primarily, it is a machine, much like the machine Marx speaks of when he defines the "State" as a machine that is driven by the juridical-legal apparatus that transforms the raw energy of class inequalities in combustion with the law and the police into a definitive form of state-power. In this case, we discover that it is an original Roman machine that takes a detour to the United States and now assumes control of the apparatus of international laws that will not only determine the meaning of public conduct and citizenship as the requisite conditions of access to territory, in the name of "security and the public peace," but will also determine the virtues of fidelity and confidence that will become conditions of access to the world market. Moreover, as a result of both determinations, henceforth all cultures will be guaranteed to have "unequal access to the same world market."[7] Following the above definition, I would like to emphasize that throughout his argument Derrida explicitly situates the concept of "faith" (*fides*, though the relationship to *pistis* would need to be examined later on) in its most contemporary meaning as not belonging to any theology, at least first of all, before its rhetorical flourish, but rather to an apparatus; specifically, to a calculating machine that makes a balance-sheet of faith in terms of "good faith in credit," trustworthiness particularly in the repayment of debt, respect for private property, which informs the value of human and animal life, and all other forms of confidence upon which the circulation of capital depends. Derrida lists these virtues as "the pledge of faith, the guarantee of trustworthiness, the fiduciary experience presupposed by all production of shared knowledge, the testimonial performativity engaged in all technoscientific performance as in the entire capitalistic economy [and] indissociable from it."[8]

Concerning the relationship between the two concepts of faith, *pistis* and *fides*, we should recall that Christianity was adopted as the official religion of the late Roman Empire under Constantine partly due to its tendency in promoting good business ethics, a relationship that still exists today in the practice of some Christian businesses when they display the sign of the *ichthys* above the cash register, indicating a promise of trustworthiness and fidelity (*fides*) in all transactions of capital based on the assumption of faith (*pistis*).

Turning now to the second aspect of globalatinization, as Marx discovered in his early analysis of Roman law, neither a purely juridical-legal apparatus nor a strictly economic machine of calculation can be understood to operate on their own; in fact, it only appears that these first two machines operate automatically and are driven by a kind of energy that Marx himself called "miraculous." However, since Marx, like Spinoza before him, was not one to believe in the existence of miracles, he was led to theorize the "miraculous nature" of this other machine, which is partly discursive and partly composed of "the human passions," whose entire function was precisely understood to create Gods and "Religion." This machine was partly discursive in the sense that Marx understood modern religion to be identified as a "global political rhetoric," which is to say, Ideology. Thus, according to Derrida's analysis of the same machinic phylum, globalatinization is defined as a "machine for creating gods and religions" (or, in this machine's contemporary function, for creating "the return of religion"). However, rather than returning to Marx's concept of Ideology, Derrida's primary source for this definition is the conclusion of Bergson's *Two Sources of Morality and Religion*, where Bergson identifies the universe as a "refractory mechanism, a planetary machine for creating Gods."[9] Following Bergson's statement, moreover, Derrida will speak everywhere of machines (technical machines, translating machines, techno-scientific machines, legal-juridical machines, commercial credit and banking machines, and the machines of capital), but, rather than speaking of the universe as a machine, he speaks instead of globalatinization as the planetary machine that is responsible for producing the meaning of religion today in its global setting. In other words, we find not only that what was originally a Roman then a European-colonial form of global political rhetoric has taken a detour to the United States, but also that today this rhetoric can be heard everywhere (including I might add, in China) as if it was a voice speaking to everyone from on high. It was curious enough that we had earlier found this voice to be speaking with an Anglo-American accent, which I have already noted is still a foreign language in some parts of the globe, but more curious, if not telling, that it can be heard to speak mostly (if not obsessively) of religion and about religion, to everyone, while also speaking beyond religion, as if from the horizon of a certain death of God. If this new planetary machine for creating Gods and religions is refractory today, as Derrida observes, it is because it detaches its meaning from a particular place or site in order to become globalized, and in this sense it can be said, like the word "religion" today, to have no specific original source or site, or to behave purely as a telecommunication satellite that lifts off and circulates the globe following a pre-ordained code or automatic pilot. At the same time, it's global signal broadcasts specific sites and places, certain local phenomena, certain groups and *threskeia*, certain manners of *religio* or "having scruples," even certain "bonds or ties" (*religare*): inevitably, it comes down and lands, attaching itself again to the very site of the "home" (or the familiar, *Heimlich*) and the family; it produces the meaning of "religion" in the hearts and minds of every living body on the planet today. It is by means of this double movement of incredible abstraction and, simultaneously, terrifying concreteness that the most contemporary meaning of religion detaches from "the specific place or cultural form," becoming more or less a globalized phenomenon that, in turn, reattaches itself to the country, the idiom, the literal and to everything confusedly collected today in the so-called "former first world" under the terms "identity" and "identitarian," thus marking the two moments of ex-appropriation and re-appropriation, or de-racination and en-racination, of the seemingly opposing and antagonistic currents that define the "return of religion" for all of us today.

Here, I must forego a detailed analysis of all the returns of religion, and will simply observe that in his argument Derrida appears to agree with Heidegger's earlier claim made in his "Letter on Humanism" (1949). Derrida argues that the resurgence of "religion" (the original Latin term we find in Derrida's text now up-rooted and speaking Anglo-American, perhaps even with a Texan accent) is bound up with the historical destination of a juridical-legal apparatus that must be understood in the most "European-colonial sense possible," one that was also founded upon *the first of all global political rhetorics: humanitas.* If, as Heidegger claimed earlier, "every humanism is a metaphysics or serves as the foundation of one," then what I am cautiously identifying is nothing less than a new humanism, or at least "the original and unprecedented source."[10] As Heidegger writes, "We encountered the first humanism in Rome: it therefore remains

142

a specifically Roman phenomenon."[11] Moreover, "The first humanism, Roman humanism, and every kind that has emerged from that time to the present" – here I underline the fact that Heidegger was making these remarks in 1949, just as Derrida's remarks are made prior to 9/11 – "has presupposed the most universal 'essence' of the human being to be obvious."[12] First and foremost, this first humanism assumes the form of a global political rhetoric that proclaims openly and for all the meaning of the *Homo humanus* as opposed to the *Homo barbarus* (for which today we might substitute the term *Homo terrorem*, who has succeeded *Homo barbarus* as representing the "mortal enemy" of *the form of existence of humanitas*). Secondly, in a refractory manner, this rhetoric also imposes the meaning of "religion" and "the religious" upon things it designates according to a quasi-imperial decree and its claim of sovereignty over other forms of life, including cultural life, or even biopolitical life. As Derrida writes concerning the first so-called apparatus, Roman Imperial Law was also accompanied by a global rhetoric that is historically incarnated in "the dominant juridical system and the concept of the State," as well as in the most "Latiniglobal and cederomized" rhetoric concerning the universality of a certain concept of religion that one hears around a "certain death of God."[13] "In as much as it comes from Rome, as is often the case, it would first try, and first in Europe, upon Europe, to impose surreptitiously a discourse [i.e., a global rhetoric], a culture, a politics, and a right, to impose them on all the other monotheist religions, including non-Catholic Christian religions."[14]

In the last statement, I would simply observe, Derrida sounds a lot like Voltaire. Moreover, he concludes his observations on both aspects of this apparatus today, the juridical calculating and the discursively rhetorical, with what is perhaps the most acute prognosis of the ultimate destination of the return of religion "for our times." He writes: "The task seems all the more urgent and problematic (incalculable calculation of religion for our times) as the demographic disproportion will not cease henceforth to threaten external hegemony, leaving the latter no stratagems other than internalization."[15] In quoting this passage, I underline the use of the words "hegemony" and "stratagem" to signal a theologico-political sense of war in response to what Derrida calls "a gesture of pacification," which is not a neutral word, but rather a stratagem or tactic invented by modern technological warfare. Certainly, "*we Anglo-Americans*" (that is, globally) would immediately understand that one of the etymological sources of this word first comes from the United States, and like the word "religion" can be understood as the hybridization of the original Latin *Pax*, or the contemporary meaning of *Pax Romanus*. In other words, as the horizon of globalatinization appears to encompass the entire planet, it exercises an almost complete "hegemony" over the "unprecedented and original" meaning of religion today, *leaving no place in the Sun for all the religions of Man*, particularly for those that have been found to belong to a receding horizon of past cultures or that are publicly condemned in both the local and global marketplace as "blasphemous," leaving them no other stratagem or "line of flight" than open or clandestine retreat.

What then are these stratagems of the internalization of religion? First, they definitely include all the fundamentalisms, and what Derrida calls all the various "integrisms" or their "politics," including I might add those that are grouped under the name of "identity" and "identitarian politics." These have often been described by contemporary sociologists, political scientists, and theologians alike as "globally localized reactions" (occurring also in "the developed world") to the encroaching horizon of modernization which often take the form of viral re-integrations of the earlier representatives of *threskeia, religio*, and even *religare* (including the creation of new bonds or social ties associated with the multiplication of the forms of bio-political life). But there are other stratagems of internalization, particularly "the return of religion" into the home, with the reappearance of the *pater familias* as the "head of the family," but also in the return of a phallic determination of the body (whether sexualized or racialized) in those forms of existence and faith that are found to be closest to the living body and its virulent sense of "auto-immunity." As Derrida observes, all these phenomena mask "a reaction against that with which it is partially linked: the dislocation, expropriation, delocaliza-tion, deracination, 'dis-idiomization' and dispossession (in all their dimensions, especially sexual – i.e., *phallic*) that the tele-techno-scientific machine [of globalatinization] does not fail to produce."[16] Taken together, they might even express the virulent forms of *resentment of Life* (*bios*) itself, which is no less machinic, the machines of *bios* against the machines of globalatinization. Consequently, one area I would highlight in Derrida's argument is his often brooding observations concerning "another death of God that comes to haunt the Passion that animates him," to which I will return in my conclusion, as well the frequent allusions to a certain phallic sexuality that is expressed in modern techno-scientific warfare involving rape warfare and biopolitical miscegenation, the exploding body without organs in the marketplace, all of which find their source in a certain phallic *jouissance*. Thus, if religion has no other recourse than a stratagem of internalization that touches again the phallic source of life for its inspiration, we find also that for the same reason Life itself has no recourse than to choose religion as "the most powerful form of resentment," or worse, to affirm the possibility of *radical Evil* in order to reassert its former sovereignty over Man. This possibility for the "return of religion" is as equally original and unprecedented as the return produced by its globalatinization. In this sense, as Derrida remarks, the horizon for the future of religion appears doubly divided, just as the very determination of the form of existence of faith appears today as the distinction between two mortal enemies who each grasp the very essence of life in the death of the other, as if vividly dramatizing the earlier riddle by Heraclitus: *To the bow (bios) belongs Life, but its work is Death.*

And yet, in all these phenomena, and speaking of the future, I simply want to point out one glaring contradiction that appears today in the very concept of "religion" itself. It would appear *as if* there is no "living religion" that does not belong to this receding horizon, as if the very source of religion has become bound up with "a certain death of God" that announces or proclaims his end like Nietzsche's madman. It is *as if* religion can no longer serve to preserve and to protect the dignity and the mystery of Life – the sacred, the holy (*heilig*) – but also that this vital (if not virulent) expression of life in the very creation of religion has been exhausted of all its productive powers, which Derrida identifies with the power of its auto-immunity. Consequently, we often speak of religion today only in the historical past tense, somewhat like anthropologists will speak of past cultures, as if there is not the slightest expectation either on earth or in heaven for the creation of a new religion of Man springing from the prodigious power of Life itself. The source has dried up, it seems, leaving us bereft of inspiration, which in my view is quite remarkable. To express this directly: Is there either space or time

146

for us to imagine the coming of a new Christ, much less a new Paul; a new Buddha or Krishna? In fact, we do not even need to imagine a "return of religion" that would take the form of these world-historical personalities, but simply to imagine the coming of a certain cult, the invention of new rituals, the creation of new scruples that would yet be without a name, or would not go under the officially sanctioned name of "religion," according to an older cederomized term. Not yet, or no longer, it seems. Recalling Bergson's statement that the universe is a machine for creating Gods, the fact that this machine no longer continues to be productive in this fashion means that either it has been left idling or found to be out of use, has been superseded by newer machines, or has been condemned by a global political rhetoric as fundamentally despotic, and for this reason represents a biopolitical threat to the security of the species.

This might prepare us to understand a third stratagem of the internalization of religion, which concerns the recourse to its essence or ground, to claim the structure of all religiosity. In other words, in what way do the recent proclamations concerning "a religion at the end of religions" or a "religion without religion" belong to what Derrida identifies as a certain double horizon of the "death of God"? One that proclaims the end of religion, narrowly defined by its historical incarnations (by its *threskeia*), but at the same time evangelizes the "good news" of an ultimate horizon, or at least, as has been said, a metaphysical clearing of the ground that will precede the breaking of a new horizon. This second horizon has been determined in terms of an "auto-deconstruction" of an earlier Christian construction, as the opening of its first sense that has overdetermined its own historical horizon, "which undoes the horizontality of sense and makes it pivot into a verticality of the present instant like an infinite breakthrough."[17] Rather than turning to Nancy's proclamation concerning "a Christianity that *would be* nihilism and has not ceased engaging nihilism, the Death of God," which Derrida would identify as yet another "self-destructive affirmation of religion," I would identify this with the source of the Christian horizon itself – at least, according to Benveniste's account. Recalling the "etymological and logical scandal" that Derrida also recounts in his reading of Benveniste, we need to pay attention to a particularly Christian genealogy that belongs to this early episode, one that fundamentally determines, according to Benveniste's subtle argument, the first encroachment of a specifically Christian horizon of meaning that still determines our sense of religion as *re-ligio* (as bond, or obligation). Accordingly, what was formerly determined as an essentially subjective disposition (that of "having scruples," an inhibition with regard to action, which could be ritualized in observance of certain moral prohibitions), henceforth becomes an objective propriety ascribed to certain things or to an ensemble of beliefs and practices. It is this objective aspect, referring to a particular set of beliefs and practices, which would undergo further systemization and codification, allowing one set of beliefs to be distinguished from another by its external practices, later identified as other religions, marking the advent of the modern horizon of the meaning of "religion" proper. As Benveniste further argues, this entails not just a transformation of the etymological sense of *religio*, but even more crucially, *"it is the very content of religio that has changed."*[18] It is here that we find the exact moment of the scandal that Derrida points to, since it would appear that, according to Benveniste, it is not simply that the word underwent a diachronic semantic alteration in which its earlier meaning could co-exist alongside its new signified,

but rather that it was subject to a complete synchronic transformation in which one signified was replaced by another and
organized hierarchically (if we are to understand that this is what
Benveniste means by "content"). What is this new signified, and
how is it specifically found to be a Christian invention? "For a
Christian," Benveniste writes,

> what characterizes this new faith, in relation to pagan cults,
> is the bond of piety, this dependence of fidelity in relation to
> God, this *obligation* in the proper sense of the word. Thus the
> concept of *religio* is remodeled upon the idea that the human
> makes of his relation to God; an idea that is totally different
> from the old roman *religio* and one that prepares for its modern
> sense (*acception*).[19]

If we accept Benveniste's argument concerning the horizon of
a specifically Christian sense of *religio*, one that will prefigure
its modern senses, as being bound up with the substitution of
external obligation for subjective scruples, then what would be
the implications of this total semantic transformation? First of
all, since obligation is defined as the state of being "bound to the
oath" objectively determined by a set of beliefs and practices, the
existence of religion will henceforth be determined by the degree
to which it can create obligation and the manner in which it
commands obedience. Here, I would recall that the entire premise
of Benveniste's analysis is to explain how what was formerly a
purely subjective disposition found in all early Indo-European
societies, including Persia, representing all manners of religious
scruples and cultic expressions of the sacred, gives way, after the
Roman recognition of Christianity as the official and "authentic
cult" set against the various illegitimate "superstitions," to the
emergence of religion as a distinct and separate social institution

that is co-determinate with the evolution of the State-Form. At the very beginning of his analysis, Benveniste writes: "If it is in fact true that religion is an institution, this institution has not always been separated from others, nor positioned outside of them. We will be able to conceive of this clearly and thus define religion only at the moment when it is delimited, and where its domain is distinct."[20] It is this emergence as a separate institution that is also prefigured by the transformation of the sense of *religio*, which is stated both as a problem of etymology and as signaling a fundamental transformation of Indo-European institutions. (As Derrida also points out, almost all of Benveniste's conclusions show how the etymological aberrations of late Roman society fatally determined the path of Western social and political ideas, producing any number of logical scandals that cannot so easily be explained.) Secondly, following from the emergence of religion as a "distinct and separate domain" characterized by a subjective form of obligation that passes for belief and, externally, by "a set of beliefs and practices" that are themselves obligatory in nature, it becomes inevitable that this institution will enter into strife and conflict with other powers for determining subjective obligations, such as the family, or even the institutions of the State itself, particularly with the emergence of state-sponsored obligations surrounding "the Rights of Man," the modern and authentic cult of humanism belonging to late democratic Christian societies, which continues to be responsible for bringing the era marked by the power of religious institutions to a point of intense crisis.

In the above, I have outlined the major aspects of Benveniste's overall argument in order to make the following observation: If the original sense that determines the Christian horizon of the word religion is bound up with the transformation of its semantic content, supplanting subjective scruples with external obligations, it is crucial to note that most of the recent "self-destructive affirmations of religion" have been remodeled on the idea of a sense of de-obligation, or a de-propriation of the term's signified content. In other words, rather than opening out to the ontological ground of the structure of religiosity as such, many of these arguments only perform a suspension or "bracketing" of the Christian sense of *faith as obligation*, that is, the specific-ally Christian content of the word religion that belongs to its first horizon, and may not touch again on the concept's other meanings. These have also continued to circulate indiscrimin-ately throughout postmodern societies, including the more archaic sense of "having scruples" which can also be found in any number of social and political practices today, such as ecological movements that promote new inhibitions and strict collective observances with regard to the environment. The fact that these new practices and behaviors are, for the most part, not the expressions of a separate social institution or "apparatus" (*dispositive*), which would codify them into a set of beliefs and obligatory observances, is a further reflection of the weakening of the sense of *religio*, or rather, of the return of another sense of religion that, as Benveniste defines it, "indicates an internal disposition and not an objective propriety or systematized set of beliefs and practices."[21]

As another sign of the weakening of this sense of *religio* belonging to the first (Christian) horizon, I return again to the more recent "self-destructive affirmations of religion" that have occurred mostly in Christian theology and philosophy, within the most developed (and the richest) countries globally, even though, as Derrida has remarked, the Pope has also participated in the proclamation of a certain "death of God" theology. Although no longer claiming the status of a science, postmodern Christian theology still retains a function of the codification and hierarchical arrangement of the ontic and ontological attributes of religion, that is, an *orthodoxical* function it has inherited from its earlier roles in relation to the apparatus of the Church, as well as the class perspective represented by theologians and philosophers (as was pointed out early on by Maimon in the eighteenth century). In other words, although lacking any relation to a distinct domain or apparatus, or even to a clear and distinct set of beliefs and practices, it still retains a form of orthodoxy even when this is expressed in the most abstract and metaphysical discourse devoid of all objectively religious content, even though this discourse leaves intact a place for purely subjective expressions of piety and fidelity. I have already observed the suspension or "bracketing" of the sense of obligation in the definition of religion imparted by many of these discourses (though they still retain what Derrida calls "the most Latinoglobal and cederomized" of rhetoric), but equally absent is any accompanying sense of social obligation attached to the new horizon of religion, which could even be described as "anti-communitarian" in its emphasis on negative community. I will not engage in polemics as to whether this or that particular thinker is guilty of this expression, since it is general enough to remark a certain trend in theological thinking today. Instead, what interests me is the manner in which Derrida elliptically reads the claims for a weakened sense of *religio* as precisely the sign of an auto-immune defense against another sense with which it is fatally linked: namely, the so-called "resurgence" of more virulent expressions of auto-immune defense and biopolitical community, not by accident among the poorest populations globally. It is also not by chance that the most pronounced expressions of "negative theology" have gained popularity only in the richest countries, and here we might recall Derrida's earlier observation that the increasing demographic population that belongs to the first auto-immune defense will ultimately threaten its external hegemony of the latter, leaving this now globalized class "no stratagems other than internalization," under which we might locate the sense of internalization performed by any negative theology.[22] As Derrida writes, the "auto-immune haunts the community and its system of immune survival like the hyperbole of its own possibility."[23]

Following this final observation, perhaps as an aside, I would like to point out a striking similarity between Foucault's earlier remarks on the historical transformation of the nature of sovereignty associated with the birth of "the Rights of Man" and the emergence of what he vaguely calls "biopower" with Derrida's observation concerning what he calls a "double horizon" of the death of God, according to which the first horizon announced in "the self-destructive affirmation of religion" (which proclaims the essence of *religio* as pacifist, ecumenical or "Catholic") at the same time hides or conceals another horizon associated with a gesture of pacification, that is, with the reality of globalatin-ization itself. Therefore, Derrida challenges us to think the meaning of "the return of religion and of the religious" under both horizons, which he reminds us are always complex and overdetermined, by posing the following question: How is it possible to understand the form of absolute peace announced under the first horizon, even of a certain pacific or oceanic feeling often associated with the theological pronouncements of "religion at the end of religion" or "religion without religion," without also announcing (at least as the condition of the new horizon) the total pacification of the sense of *re-ligio* that is embodied by the term's other historical representatives, even if this would also include the pacification of the sense of *religare*, that is, of historical Christianity as well?

In concluding with the above observations, I realize that I am skirting close to the most traditional and proto-Marxist definition of Ideology, albeit between the two global classes of rich and poor and their native intelligentsia, but this is only to remind us of an earlier thesis concerning the different historical humanisms that have spread across the face of the earth (i.e., "*the genuine romanitas of homo romanus*" first of all, then, the *renascentia romanitas* of the fourteenth and fifteenth centuries in Italy, the *studium humanitas*, the eighteenth-century humanisms of Goethe, Winckelmann, and Schiller; the twentieth-century humanism of Marxism, and in a broader historical sense, the global humanism of Christianity as well). In each case, we can find a certain "double horizon of the death of God," but which can only appear from a certain angle of critique, at which point the manner in which one horizon hides or conceals another can be revealed. Therefore, could it also be argued that the recent attempts to "think God otherwise" are part of a larger movement of globalatinization that Derrida identifies as the contemporary double horizon of "the death of God." It is said to be doubled in the sense that the first horizon announcing the death of God (the death of an archaic or fundamentalist image of God as despot and absolute sovereign) is elided by another horizon that both conceals and divides the same horizon into two unequal moments, echoing the fact that both images of God actually exist in the contemporary world and define the current religious war over the form of existence that will belong to the future of the word, the thing, "religion." Following Derrida's critique of this double horizon, therefore, we might ask in what way does this most recent "self-destructive affirmation of religion" also hide or conceal the "gesture of pacification"?

Before this unprecedented "double-bind," to use Derrida's term, of an affirmation that hides or conceals its hostility toward another negative meaning, paradoxically hidden in the form of the affirmation of religion itself, we might also be reminded of an enigmatic statement once made by Deleuze: that today the Rights of Man can both preserve biopolitical life and, at the same time, authorize another holocaust. Here, in conclusion, allow me to quote a passage from Deleuze's *Foucault* (1988) which is I think also referring to the same phenomenon; although, using Foucault's language, Deleuze understands this as the transition between the death of a sovereign privilege and the emergence of a new horizon associated with the values of a disciplinary model which takes life as its object of control. "At that point," Deleuze writes,

> law increasingly renounces that symbol of sovereign privilege, the right to put someone to death (the death penalty), but allows itself to produce all the more hecatombs and genocides; not by returning to the old law of killing, but on the contrary in the name of race, precious space, conditions of life and the survival of a population that believes itself better than its enemy, which it now treats not as the juridical enemy of the old sovereign but as a toxic or infectious agent, a sort of "biological danger."[24]

In other words, from that point onward, "the death penalty tends to be abolished and holocausts grow 'for the same reasons'."[25] In commenting on this passage in relation to Derrida's reference to a "pacifying gesture" (which could also be understood implicitly to authorize another holocaust in the name of universal peace), I would point out that the qualities of "insanity" or "madness" could also be treated as biopolitical dangers, and I would consider the pages in "Faith and Knowledge" that specifically concern the double-bind of immunity and auto-immunity in religion and science to be perhaps the most acute and profound reflections on the same phenomenon that was observed earlier by Foucault under the concept of "biopolitical life." We have no better image of the renunciation of the earlier image of despotic sovereignty that is represented by two archaic fathers – first, Chronos, who ate his own children; then, Abraham, who thought it possible, even for a minute, to sacrifice the life of his son to satisfy the demand of his divine master – than the image that Derrida provides us, according to the same "gesture of pacification" and appeal to techno-scientific reason, of a new Abraham "who would henceforth refuse to sacrifice his son and would no longer envisage what was always madness."[26]

Finally, allow me to provide the portrait of this new Abraham who belongs to the contemporary horizon of the "death of God" (as Sovereign, or Absolute Master, who, by the way, no longer comes to us from Germany) by referring to the preface of John D. Caputo's *The Weakness of God: A Theology of the Event* (2006). Here Caputo reports on the religious and/or theological rationalizations that occurred in the aftermath of the tsunami that happened "on the day after Christmas 2004."

> Predictably, many religious leaders have been rushing to the nearest microphone or camera to explain that, while these are all innocent victims, we cannot hope to explain the mystery of God's ways – implying that this natural disaster is something that God foresaw but for deeper reasons known only to the divine mind chose not to foretell. Others are telling us that God has taken this terrible occasion to remind us that we are all sinners and to dish out some much needed and justifiable punishment

to the human race ... Those are blasphemous images of God for me, clear examples of the bankruptcy of the thinking of God as a strong force with power to intervene upon natural processes like the shifting movements of the crustal plates around the Pacific Rim as our planet slowly cools – the decision depending on what suits the divine plan.[27]

In reporting these "blasphemous images of God," Caputo provides the pathetic image of "a father who lost his grip on his three-year-old daughter and watched in horror as she was carried out to sea." I don't know if this image was based on actual news footage or reportage of the personal tragedies surrounding this natural disaster, but what I find interesting is the warring images of the "new Abraham" contained in this short preface to Caputo's attempt to "think of God otherwise." What are the "blasphemous images of God" that Caputo calls upon us to hastily reject? First, there is the primitive God of Nature who speaks in earthquakes, volcanoes, and floods and causes us to tremble with fear and awe (the God of terror and of terrorists). Second, there is the obscurantist God of anti-rationalistic discourses that appeal to the "mystery of God's ways," which could be associated with the Enlightenment critique of appeals to superstition and obscurantist irrationality. Finally, there is the prophetic image of God as Sovereign and Despot who enjoys an absolute biopolitical right over all living things and is free to use the death of seemingly innocent victims to proclaim the abiding truth of his Kingdom. In place of these, we are given the pathetic image of a father who helplessly witnesses his daughter's sacrifice to these insane Gods, already foregrounding the proclamation of another Abraham who will find these other Gods to be depraved and blasphemous, like the images of deranged thoughts racing through a traumatized brain, but not by any appeal to science and reason, since this recourse has also been foreclosed in the arguments that follow. Apparently, Caputo's God is also helpless to intervene in natural processes, but what interests me most is that these reflections on the aftermath of the tsunami may, in fact, conceal an anxiety about another wave coming from the same region, the rising wave of radical Islam that is approaching the first world. In facing this other wave, it would be significant to note that the portrait of the new Abraham is that of a helpless victim. Therefore, I will end my statements here with a reflection on this image in the context of Derrida's earlier observation already quoted above: "The task today seems all the more urgent and problematic (incalculable calculation of religion for our times) as the demographic disproportion will not cease henceforth to threaten external hegemony, leaving the latter no stratagems other than internalization."[28]

Notes

1 Derrida, *Perjury and Pardon*, vol. 1 (forthcoming).

2 Derrida, *On Touching: Jean-Luc Nancy*, p. 191.

3 The translated version I am referring to is primarily from Derrida and Vattimo's *Religion*. I cannot hope, nor will I even attempt, to provide as complete and detailed account of this address as has Michael Naas; consequently, I will simply refer the reader to his *Miracle and Machine: Jacques Derrida and the Two Sources of Religion, Science, and the Media* (2012).

4 Derrida and Vattimo, *Religion*, p. 69.

5 Ibid., p. 21.

6 Ibid., p. 42.

7 Ibid., p. 43.

8 Ibid., p. 44.

9 See "Static Religion," in Bergson, *Two Sources of Religion and Morality*, pp. 83ff.

10 Heidegger, *Pathmarks*, p. 244.

11 Ibid.
12 Ibid., p. 245.
13 Derrida and Vattimo, *Religion*, p. 72.
14 Ibid., p. 43.
15 Ibid.
16 Ibid., p. 45.
17 Nancy, *Dis-enclosure: The Deconstruction of Christianity*, p. 156.
18 Benveniste, *Le Vocabulaire des institutions indo-Europeennes, tome 2*, p. 272 (emphasis mine).
19 Ibid.
20 Ibid., p. 266.
21 Ibid., p. 272.
22 Derrida and Vattimo, *Religion*, p. 79.
23 Ibid., p. 82.
24 Deleuze, *Foucault*, p. 92.
25 Ibid.
26 Derrida and Vattimo, *Religion*, p. 79.
27 Caputo, *The Weakness of God*, p. xi.
28 Derrida and Vattimo, *Religion*, p. 43.

7

The Unprecedented Return of St. Paul

"The great force of Marxist philosophy, which takes its point of departure in economic man, lies in its ability to completely avoid the hypocrisy of sermons. ... One does not attribute to it the second thoughts of deceivers, dupes, or the sated." – Emmanuel Levinas, *Existence and Existents* (1947)

The well-known conceptual relationship between crisis (*krisis*) and critique (*krinein*) in post-Kantian philosophy is perhaps most forcefully pronounced in the philosophy of Husserl. Of course, philosophy has been in a crisis for some time, if not from the very beginning, and if we recall that the Greek *polis* amounted to less than a thousand citizens, referring only to the members of the civil assembly (*ekklesia,* later translated as "church"), which was smaller than the average Greek village, we might conclude that, quantitatively speaking, the demographic population of philosophers on this earth has not increased that much since the time of the Greeks, despite their historical migration into the urban centers of modernity. The question I will ask here is whether the contemporary crisis announced under the terms of the "post-secular" or the "return to religion" is remarkably different than the earlier crisis between philosophy and the positive sciences announced by Husserl in 1936, and even earlier, the crisis between reason and faith in the period of the Enlightenment. In taking up this question – what is this post-secular crisis all about? – I will turn to examine the recent writings of the contemporary French philosopher Alain Badiou on the emblematic figure of St. Paul.

Concerning this "return statement," my argument will be that "the return of Paul" on the contemporary scene, spurred on by the recent readings of the Pauline figure by Agamben and Badiou (and by Žižek, to a lesser degree), represents a post-secular – i.e., post-scientific – response to the perceived crisis of philosophical subjectivity that has emerged alongside the decline of what has gone under the name of "Critical Theory" (or simply "theory") in North America and elsewhere (in short, the anti-humanist traditions of, primarily, German and French philosophy). However, what I am defining as "post-secular," in this moment, does not simply refer to the phenomenon of fundamentalism in religion alone, but also occurs when the subject of philosophy is grounded in something resembling a "form of faith" and no longer on a scientific principle of reason, which has been reduced in the postmodern period to being one "fable" among others (i.e., ideology). This does not mean that all philosophy thereby becomes religious, or nostalgically assumes a pious stance with regard to the world (although this has certainly happened), but rather concerns the manner in which philosophy assumes a subjective form of certainty concerning its own truth-claims in contradistinction to the truth-procedures of the other sciences.

First, let us recall our earlier discussion of Heidegger's claim that philosophy is not opposed to theology, but rather to faith as "a subjective form of existence."[1] This is because, for Heidegger, philosophy is "factically ever-changing" whereas he understands religious faith as the inward or subjective form of existence that is characterized by something like permanent conviction, or belief (*pistis*). In other words, the philosopher's convictions are historically ever-changing because philosophers constantly change their minds about philosophy's own truth-procedures (to employ Badiou's term), and this is especially evident in the case of the procedures invented by earlier philosophers, which undergo constant revision. By contrast, for Heidegger, the form of existence defined by faith is founded upon a set of firm convictions that are impervious (or at the very least resistant and sometimes openly hostile) to a complete "transformation of mind" (*metanoia*) that appears as the historical condition of philosophy's ever-changing appearance, since such a change would also necessarily imply the destruction of the subject (of faith), that is, the subjective core of a belief-system. Therefore, to change one's faith entails something more radical than a mere change in opinion, since while the truth of propositions may change over time, this does not require the complete "destruction" of the Subject (*subiectum*) that underlies them. Again, it is for this reason that Heidegger claims that faith is the "mortal enemy" (*todfeind*) of the form of existence that is called philosophy.[2]

In the contemporary moment, however, it seems that it is the factically ever-changing nature of truth claims that now appears as the entire problem of philosophy's own subjective form of existence and authority, especially in light of the ever-changing, multiple, and shifting identities belonging to globalized societies (to paraphrase a refrain often made by Žižek). Today, philosophy appears bereft of the power to brand its own truth-claims with the stamp of the Real that was formerly provided by its earlier claim to the idea of Reason, or by its adherence to a form of scientific

162

method, as in the case of phenomenology. Even in the so-called postmodern period, the appeal to a Structuralist method, or to the "logic of the Signifier," still assumed the epistemological form of a "Science of the Subject," especially in psychoanalysis and Althusserian Marxism. It is in this context, perhaps, that we might approach the work of Badiou, who resolves to transform the subjective form of philosophy by exchanging the principle of reason for a firmer foundation of faith (or what I would posit as a post-secular form of "conviction" which is not religious in principle). For Badiou, moreover, this gesture represents the "heroic" effort to vindicate the militant subjectivity of Marxist-Leninist critique against competing truth-procedures, especially those that have been formulated most successfully in Europe and the United States in the contemporary period by feminist and minority critiques under the banner of what he will call a Levinasian "ethics of difference," which I will return to discuss below.[3]

But first, why Paul? How does Pauline Christianity provide a foundation for the new universalism proclaimed by an atheist and Marxist philosopher like Badiou? Although at first glance this might appear somewhat paradoxical, the answer will be found in the implicit parallelism between the "Christ-event" proclaimed by Paul in the first century C.E. and the truth-event of Marx proclaimed by Badiou, which can only be understood by subtracting, as a condition of this claim, any reference to an historical reality or "objective aggregate" of facts. Some of these facts would include the role played by former Eastern European churches in the historical defeat of communism and the subsequent reappraisal of religious activism by South American Liberation Theologians. To this I would only add the global causes and consequences that precipitated and followed

163

the collapse of the former Soviet Union, in particular the political bankruptcy and gradual "senilization" of any remaining Marxist-Leninist or Maoist regimes, which only appear as what Althusser called "survivals" (*survivants*) in a world increasingly ruled by neoliberal principles of "governmentality" (Foucault).

In the context of Badiou's own argument, given the parallelism that he finds between our contemporary world and the world of the first century C.E., the truth-procedure invented by Paul to establish the subjective foundation of a universalist identity (i.e., an identity without any "identitarian character-istics") in response to his own political and cultural situation, may provide the necessary strategy to guarantee the survival of his own "critical" position in contemporary neoliberal society, especially in view of the role played by the United States in his cosmic allegory. "Paul's unprecedented gesture," Badiou writes, "consists in subtracting truth from the communitarian grasp, be it that of a people, a city, an empire, a territory, or a social class."[4] Likewise, in order to avoid being defeated on the basis of "mere facts," our contemporary militant philosopher must first devise a method of subtracting his own truth-procedure from any current historical circumstances in establishing its claim of proof, or certainty, since it is faith (or rather, "conviction") and not reason that also grasps the nature of the truth-event as a subjective form of existence, "*an event whose only 'proof' lies in its having been declared by a subject.*"[5]

What, then, is the so-called "truth-procedure" invented by Paul that Badiou reduces, on the one hand, to an "unprecedented gesture" (a pure act without foundation in previous tradition) and, on the other hand, to a "pure element of Saying" (*pointe de fable*)? Certainly, Paul's original gesture consists of subtracting the entire narrative of the historical Jesus of Nazareth (including the narrative of the life of Jesus given in the Gospels, as well as everything that Jesus said) and in reducing the "Christ-event" to one pointed Saying: "Jesus is resurrected!"[6] Of course, this "pure element of Saying" cannot be understood philosophically as a proposition, as Badiou rightly observes, but rather in the strongest sense as a proclamation of *faith in the event* (which would not be accurately captured as "belief" in the usual sense accorded to the Greek word *pistis*). At the same time, as a self-proclaimed atheist, Badiou does not merely seek to repeat the content of Paul's original statement either, since the reality of the resurrected Christ is declared to be a "fiction" according to the secondary meaning of *fabula*, as he defines it, a residue that still clings to the pure element of Saying and is mediated by the Imaginary.[7] Stripped of its "fabulous content" therefore, and "unburdened by all the imaginary that surrounds it," what is retained is only the pure element of the Saying itself. Although the form of this faith is certainly "religious" (and it is philosophical only in its own unique "fable") it is consciously a religious form stripped of its religious "fable" (i.e., its fiction or genre, as a form of Saying), one in which "conviction" replaces "faith" (*pistis*), the subject of militant conviction replaces the subject of love (*agape*, or charity), and the subjective form of "certainty" replaces "hope" (*elpis*).[8]

What exactly is this element? Again, it is the unprecedented and heterogeneous nature of the "truth-event" first introduced by Paul not only as a form of thought but also as the act of declaring the truth of this thought, which is violently posed against two other world-views – the Greek and the Jewish moral universes – from which Paul struggles to extricate the meaning of a Christian form of existence. As Early Christian scholar Wayne A. Meeks writes: "The novelty of the proclamation [saying, *pointe de fable*], which violates or at least transcends expectations based on either reason or on Jewish traditions (1 Cor. 1:18–25), *permits it to serve as a warrant for innovation*."[9] In this regard, Badiou is completely accurate in his reading of the meaning of the statement "Jesus is resurrected!" as a radical departure from both moral and philosophical systems that renders the subjective element of a distinctively Christian "life" (*zoe*), one that is "indifferent" (in a word) to the former determinations of the flesh (*sarx*) under Jewish law, and to the natural predisposition of things and persons to come or "to return to their own place" according to Greek wisdom. The event proclaimed by Paul could never exist in either universe, which becomes the basis for the heterogeneity of the Christian form of existence as a new determination of Life (*zoe*), no longer predicated on the previous ethnological and cultural characteristics of kinship and class. As Meeks writes, "In particular, Paul uses the paradox of the Messiah's crucifixion explicitly to support the union of Jew and gentile and the abolition of the distinction between them, by bringing to an end the boundary setting function of the Torah."[10]

In his own argument, Badiou employs the Pauline "paradox" as the foundation for a new form of universalism, defined as a militant subjective form of a radical "indifference that tolerates differences." In other words, he uses the "unprecedented gesture" of Paul as a precedent (as one also says in jurisprudence) to found his own gesture on another fable – the revolutionary fable of the truth-event first proclaimed by Marx. It is around this point, however, that the explicit parallelism Badiou seeks to establish between the heroic (and fanatical) subject of Paul, who proclaims the truth-event of the resurrected Christ, and the subject of "he who proclaims the pure event" (i.e., the subject of Badiou himself?) becomes overtly contrived, which is one reason why Badiou elides in his account the second part of the Pauline saying: "Christ is Lord" (meaning also that all Christians are to be understood as "slaves to Christ").

I have already established above the two senses of the "fable" by which Badiou determines the "Christ-event" of St. Paul as an allegorical means of addressing the situation of crisis in contemporary philosophy. Of course, allegory is a type of fable often employed in moral philosophy, which Badiou's own discourse unquestioningly is. How we know it is allegorical is explicitly stated in the "situation" to which this discourse is addressed, when Badiou writes that Paul's original discourse speaks directly *to us* from out of the same conditions, namely, the increasing despotism and militarism of the Roman Empire, which is represented *in our time* by the United States. By transplanting Paul, along with all his statements, into our century, they encounter a real society every bit as criminal and corrupt as, but infinitely more supple and resistant than, that of the Roman Empire.[11] Moreover, in his own allegorical identification with the figure of St. Paul, Badiou also might also appear to us today as "heroic," "fanatical," or even as a "zealot." Simply put, Paul was a self-styled zealot for Christ in the same manner that Badiou remains a zealot for Lenin and Mao, and particularly against those who would declare such a conviction to be a "folly" given the evidence against this system of belief and the disappearance of the peoples that marked its historical existence. However, it is only in the peculiar sense of heroism employed by Badiou to describe his own "situation" vis-à-vis that of Paul that the saying "Jesus is resurrected!" is given its true meaning as allegory.

Returning now to Badiou's appropriation of the original Pauline argument that "there is no distinction between Greek and Jew," *this argument is only valid if we also fully accept the following claim as a condition*: that the "new type of subject" proclaimed by Badiou, "for him who considers that the real is pure event," fulfills and at the same time "cancels out" the reality of all ethnic and cultural identity in the same manner that, for Paul, Christ came to fulfill and thereby to satisfy the laws of the Torah, bringing them to closure through the inauguration of a new subject for whom the continued recognition of ethnic and cultural differences would now have an anachronistic and "backward" meaning.[12] In other words, declaring the nondifference of Greek and Jew establishes Christianity's potential universality; to found the Subject as division, rather than as the perpetuation of a tradition, renders the subjective element adequate to this universality by terminating the predicative particularity of cultural subjects. "There is no doubt that universalism, and hence the existence of any truth whatsoever, *requires the destitution of established differences* and the initiation of a subject divided in itself by the challenge of having nothing but the vanished event to face up to."[13] It is only upon assuming the full reality of this event, or this universal "subjective void," that the subject is capable of "radical indifference," in the face of which all identities will henceforth appear as fictions, opinions of culture and tradition, including the very phenomenal appearance of racial and sexual characteristics, which are henceforth regarded as the fictive projections of the Imaginary. Here, and in many other statements, Badiou actually reveals himself to be gnostic in his attitude; thus, the cancellation of the reality of cultural, racial, and sexual difference is based on a prior denial of the reality of this world, which is ruled by chaos and by demons. It is crucial to note here that for Badiou, as for Paul, the greatest evil is belief in multiple identities, since this poses the greatest threat to the potential universality of the Subject. Multiple identities are the little "daemons" that rule in chaos; as Paul says, "one cannot drink from the cup of Christ and the cup of demons at the same time" (that is, without contamination).

It is around this final point that Badiou's identification of Levinas as the founder of a neoliberal "ethics of difference" also becomes somewhat contrived, if not a form of calculated subreption. Why Levinas? Why does Levinas's ethical philosophy appear as the object of Badiou's most fervent critiques from 1993 onward, as the real antagonist and opponent, in an almost identical manner to Paul's condemnation of "the Teacher" in the letter to the Galatians, whom he accuses of preaching "a fraudulent gospel"?[14] In answering this question, we can say of the Badiou-Levinas relation what Badiou himself often says of the Nietzsche-Paul relation: that the latter figure is more like a rival than a real enemy. The most critical difference between Badiou's and Levinas's philosophical systems only appears in a statement at the end of *Saint Paul*, where Badiou declares "that in order for people to be gripped by truth, it is imperative that universality not present itself under the aspect of particularity."[15] This argument is made even more explicit in the passage that follows, and it provides the very basis for the rhetorical strategy all along, against the claim that universalism, conceived as the production of the Same, found its emblem, if not its culmination, in the death camps, where everyone, having been reduced to a body on the verge of death, was absolutely equal to everyone else. This "argument," Badiou insists, is fraudulent.[16]

Of course, Badiou's criticisms of this clichéd understanding of Christian universalism as being entirely responsible for the holocaust and for the reduction of all political life to "bare life" are correct. In particular, the camps were responsible for introducing completely new and exorbitant differences between absolute death and bare life into our "civilization" as actual, and not merely possible, forms of social and political existence – and they continue to remain a real possibility for our political forms today and in the future (that is, unless one believes that it is no longer possible to use genocide as a political weapon). Secondly, the Pauline formula of Christian universalism (based on the fusion of community through love) cannot be reduced to Nazi "exceptionalism," based on the exclusion and extermination of difference from a community understood as a "closed substance, continuously driven to verify its own closure, both in and outside itself, through carnage."[17] Nevertheless, the implication that the ethical thought of Levinas, as perhaps the most systematic contemporary critique of "the production of the Same," is the origin of this point of view is also a type of fraud, or, at the very least, a false testimony perpetrated by Badiou himself. Strategically, as I noted above, it constitutes a form of "subreption," which, according to an older usage, involves the deliberate misstatement of facts in order to gain an ecclesiastical advantage.

First, let us again recall that, according to the etymology of the word in both Jewish and Greek systems, a fable is "saying" (*logos*, *legein*). For Levinas, however, the pure element of "Saying" (*Dire*) is expressed in a manner that cannot be reduced to "the said" (*le dit*), and thus it also remains heterogeneous to every attempt to totalize its sense within an order of nature or reason. It is in this sense of a heterogeneity already accorded to the pure element of the "truth-event" that, as we have seen, Badiou perceives the ethical fable of Levinas as the most powerful rival to his own that goes under the name of Paul:

> *For Paul*, the Christ-event is heterogeneous to the law, pure excess over every prescription, grace without concept or appropriate rite. The real can no more be what in elective

exception becomes literalized in stone as timeless law (Jewish discourse), than what comes or returns to its place (Greek discourse) ... *For him* who considers that the real is pure event, Jewish and Greek discourses no longer present, *as they continue to do in the work of Levinas, the paradigm of a major difference in thought.* This is the driving force behind Paul's universalist conviction: that "ethnic" or cultural difference, of which the opposition between Greek and Jew is in his time and in the empire as a whole, the prototype, is no longer significant with regard to the real, or to the new object that sets out a new discourse. *No real distinguishes the first two discourses any longer, and their distinction collapses into rhetoric.*[18]

In the above passage I have placed emphasis on the surreptitious replacing of the subject in the statement, "*For him* who considers that the real is pure event," which no longer refers to Paul, nor even to the "Christ-event," which is merely a fable, but again to the subject of the pure universal event of the Real without mediation. Here, we find the philosophy of Levinas defined as representing a uniquely contemporary synthesis of both Jewish and Greek discourses as "the paradigm of a major difference in thought," that is, as the ethical foundation for the ideology of the "right to difference" and what Badiou refers to as the "con-temporary catechism of goodwill with regard to 'other cultures' (i.e., multi-culturalism)."[19] To put it crudely, in the manner of Badiou, Levinas's ethical philosophy is responsible for what in the United States has gone under the name of "identity politics," and in France, from the early 1990s onward, for the political appeals based on the recognition of the rights of immigrant groups and other social minorities.

According to the terms of Badiou's own argument, however, we would need to affirm that Levinas's ethical philosophy has actually been successful in overturning the Greek *logos* by supplanting ontological difference with ethical difference, thereby introducing a new position of "Critique" into the contemporary philosophical genre. For Levinas, as we know, difference is incarnated in "the face," which is anterior to the self-reflexive identity of the ego with the other, either as the co-existence of two terms in a "logical unity," or in the form of a "transcendental apperception" of an ultimate intentionality. Therefore, ethical difference can only be phrased in the accusative mode, which is derived from an intersubjective space that is primordially asymmetrical; it is only in this manner that difference is introduced as severely restricting the ego's own freedom and self-presence, thereby making possible the two poles of obsession (*eros*) and nihilation (*abaddon*). However, in order to understand Badiou's claim that a Levinasian conception of difference functions as "the paradigm of a major difference in thought," we would first need to translate the above concepts into the form of a truth-procedure that would illustrate the concept of difference enacted by all forms of "identitarian politics" today. Accordingly, the concept of difference is enacted or produced by something like the following truth-procedure:

1. Difference is introduced from the "position" of an other who is determined in the pure element of Saying, in the epiphany of a face, a "position" that expresses the essential asymmetry and exteriority of all social relations.
2. Difference is expressed in the form of an accusative that is addressed to the sovereign and a-temporal position of the "I," thereby making this Subject "responsible to" the very condition of exteriority and alterity of the other (often described by Levinas in terms of privation of being or poverty).

172

3. The Saying (*le Dire*) of Difference becomes the formal occasion of a truth-procedure and the "conversion" of the other into another subject (in the act of self-nomination), and thus, all subsequent truth-procedures belonging to the name of the particular difference (*le dit*) become the basis for the positive construction of both subjective knowledge and social being (*conatus*).

Although this very schematic portrayal of a common truth-procedure can easily be recognized in many critical identity claims (those of ethnic minorities, for example, or in the history of feminist critique), we should immediately recall Badiou's admission that this schema "is strikingly distant from Levinas's actual conception of things."[20] In point of fact, Levinas would regard the third step in the truth-procedure outlined above as merely another instance of "the return into the Same," whereby "one signifies the other and is signified by it," and the one and the other become the co-existence of two terms in the same theme, despite their actual difference. For example, this often occurs when identity enters as a third term (e.g., a name) that mediates the one and the other in a common theme, immersing the co-implication of different subjective and temporal instances "in a collective representation, a common ideal, or a common action."[21]

From his earliest work *Existence and Existents* (1947) onwards, Levinas does argue that the space of thought cannot be separated, be considered in isolation, or even appear as the epiphenomenal distance from social space (as in writing), in as much as the epi-phenomenon of alterity that conditions the appearance of thought in writing is first introduced by the relationship to others. In other words, the ego, as subject, cannot endow itself with its own alterity, its own temporal nothingness, that is, with the scintillating alteration of presence and absence that first gives it the freedom to pull back from its engagement with the world without being able withdraw completely. It is the original alterity of the other that first creates this freedom and temporality as a possibility of existence, even though this freedom can only exist *in relation* to the world of others. Otherwise, Levinas asks, "how could time arise in a solitary subject?"

> The solitary subject cannot deny itself; it does not possess nothingness ... This alterity comes to me only from the other. Therefore, is not sociality something more than the source of our representation of time: is it not time itself? ... The dialectic of time is the very dialectic of the relationship with the other, that is, a dialogue which has to be studied in terms other than those of the solitary subject. The dialectic of the social relationship will furnish us with a set of concepts of a new kind. And the nothingness necessary to time, which the subject cannot produce, comes from the social relationship.[22]

In this passage we might find, in much plainer terms, the entire trajectory of Levinas's subsequent project, as well as a much clearer justification for the precedence of the "ethical relation" over the ontological, according to a statement that appears later on that "ethics precedes ontology." It is this rich formulation, which unfortunately has been taken up in the most threadbare and philosophically naïve manner by many contemporary readers of Levinas, that will provide the basis for Badiou's accusation that it has become the "major paradigm of difference in thought" for ethnic and cultural expressions of particularism.

At this point, I will make two preliminary remarks that run contrary to Badiou's own conception of all things "Levinasian." Firstly, at least at this stage of the phenomenological argument, there is little to suggest that Levinas is attempting to erect a purely religious understanding of ethics in place of a Greek and philosophical system, much less, that the origin of this understanding must be located in Jewish law. Secondly, there is even less evidence for what Badiou labels an ideological and culturalist assumption of multiculturalism, of identity politics, or of an ethical particularism that refuses to tolerate real differences and seeks to suppress them under a neoliberal form of universalism. Perhaps one could argue that the primacy of both a theological representation of "the Other" and of the characteristics of Jewish exceptionalism become features of Levinas's later works, which depart from an earlier phenomenological understanding of these as themes. For Levinas, who was Jewish, the concept of a pre-original anteriority of the "Other" could be called "religious," that is, "if the term itself did not also carry the risk of becoming theological."[23] However, in the earlier work Levinas already defines this anteriority strictly in terms of the dialectic of the social relationship (which is equally a dialectic of temporality); at this point, it is only the social relationship that "will furnish us with a set of concepts of a new kind."[24]

In fact, Levinas would include the representations of theology among the "hypostases of the Ego," which fundamentally distort and cover over the initial asymmetrical character of all social relations (for example, between the child and the parent, or between genders, which becomes the focus of the subsequent work *Totality and Infinity* [1961]). In both the earlier and the later works, in his analysis of the relationships brought about by Eros as a "pathos of distance in proximity" where the asymmetrical nature of this duality of beings is maintained, Levinas will also locate the primary asymmetrical relationship between the enemy and the friend as a key political concept in which the asymmetrical formations belonging to racism and ethnocentrism will be determined as well. Thus, in the same but opposite way that the failure of communication in love constitutes the presence of the other *qua* other as an object of obsession and desire, equally the failure of communication in hostility and warfare constitutes the presence of the stranger *qua* enemy as the object of impersonal hatred and derision. In both subjective states, the other appears as the one who holds me hostage and persecutes me, and in the case of the latter, the ego can only hope to escape by fusing its own being with the anonymous and impersonal power of the collective, the group, the nation, the people, or the race. "To this collectivity of comrades," Levinas writes early on, "we contrast the I-you collectivity which precedes it. It is not participation in a third term – intermediate person, truth, dogma, work, profession, interest, dwelling, or meal; that is, it is not communion."[25]

Here, given the explicit reference to the "common meal" and "communion" in this passage – that is, the Christian and subsequently modern notions of "participation in the common" (*metaxia*) – I must return now to provide some historical context for these criticisms by supplying their direct object. The primary object of Levinas's critique in *Existence and Existents* is Heidegger's analytic of *Dasein*, with its emphasis upon the solitary states of *ek-static* temporality in the experiences of boredom, anxiety, and dread – that is, the existential states of nothingness and nihilation of being that Levinas argues are neither primordial, nor even "ontological," forms of negation and nothingness. Again, this would presuppose that the solitary subject, subtracted from all social space or intersubjective relations, would be capable of giving to itself the form of alterity (i.e., non-being), which is to say, the subjective form of time itself.

Our relationship with others is the source of our own internal consciousness of time, and it is the presence of others that is responsible for introducing the nothingness from which the dynamism of the "I" (the Subject) appears in the very exigency of the present to return; although the ego is fundamentally passive in relation to this dynamism and this exigency, and the solitary subject can only "sleep, perchance, dream, to shuffle off its mortal coil." In the simplest terms, without any hint of spiritualism or divinity, it is the particular alterity of the other that first gives the ego the possibility of non-being, both the origin and the limit of its inalienable freedom as a subject, which, contrary to an entire tradition of philosophy, the subject cannot give to itself – not even in the form of a transcendental subjectivity of the non-I, of a System or Structure, or of History. (Thus, if there is any particularism in the other, it cannot be embodied in a subject or identity.) It is the concrete presence of others that first "positions" the subject, but it is also the non-identity of the other with the ego that first gives the subject the "freedom to withdraw from others"; however, as we have already seen, even the hope in community is only a temporal withdrawal and forgetting of this primordial "position." Thus, paradoxically, the idea of fusion that informs the "we" of collectivity around a common object, a work, or a third term, is always in danger of forgetting and potentially betraying the social relation to others, later defined by Levinas in terms of passivity (which is not simply passive), vulnerability (which is not merely emotional), and responsibility (which is not only moral).

In some ways, the priority Levinas accords to the relationship to the other as primary form of alterity (of the splitting of the subject and the ego) shares many of the same principles as the psychoanalytic critique of the subject, and I would only recall the prominence given to both paternity and gender in the subsequent studies as the primary forms of intersubjectivity. More rigorously understood, therefore, the statement that ethics precedes ontology must be interpreted as follows. "Intersubjective space is initially asymmetrical," Levinas writes:

> The exteriority of the other is not an effect of space, which keeps separate what conceptually is identical, nor is there some difference in the concepts which would manifest itself through spatial exteriority. It is precisely inasmuch as it is irreducible to these two notions of exteriority that social exteriority is an original form of exteriority that takes us beyond the categories of unity and multiplicity which are valid for things [i.e., the primacy of social exteriority takes us beyond ontology], that is, are valid in the world of an isolated subject, a solitary mind. Intersubjectivity is not simply the application of the category of multiplicity to the domain the mind [i.e., "the One-All," and ironically, here we have a good approximation of the principle thesis of Badiou's ontology]. It is brought about by Eros, where in the proximity of another the distance is wholly maintained, a distance whose pathos is made up of this proximity and this duality of beings.[26]

In the above statement we are given the explicit connection between ontology, the solitary subject (or cogito), and a world deprived or forgetful of others. Consequently, ontology is a world without others, and can only exist from the perspective of a solitary subject, of the philosopher who manages (even if only temporarily or by creating a "fable") to withdraw from the world that is populated by other people, or to dream of the "fusion of egos" in the communion of community. As an aside, is not Badiou also our most solitary philosopher today?

Levinas developed these arguments between 1940 and 1945, while he was a prisoner in the German concentration camp at Hanover; during the same period, several members of his family were exterminated in concentration camps in his native Lithuania. Given this historical political context, his rejection of the Heideggerian analytic of *Dasein*, and particularly his severe criticism of the *Mitsein-andersein* formulation in *Being and Time* ("a collectivity of the *with*, and *around* truth" in an authentic form), are telling. Here, we must ask, what would be the implicit relationship between the existential and solitary moods privileged in the earlier Heidegger and the *Mitsein-andersein* privilege of the authentic community of the German *Volk* that belongs to the same period of the philosopher's work and biography? Extending Levinas's critique of the solitary subject who cannot give nothingness to itself, from out of its own substance, can a people (or a race) give to itself its own creative nothingness, which in turn will give birth to its unity in an ideal future? If only by implication, Levinas suggests that this is only possible through a violent denial of the primordial relationship to "others," by a frenzied pathos for the creation of a "proximity in distance," by an Eros borne from the ideal of fusion that belonged to National Socialism at this moment.

Finally, it is obvious that according to Marxist dogma there is only one authentic species (*Geshlecht*) of social relationship that determines the asymmetrical organization of intersubjective social space, that is, "the final instance" and prior to all other forms of asymmetry: the class relationship. In view of this "authentic" social form of asymmetry, all other species of inequality (between genders, ethnic groups, minorities), as well as the different subjects of human rights, are fraudulent and "imaginary" projections of false consciousness produced by the ideological machines controlled by the masters. (In this regard, Badiou, like Žižek, is extremely orthodox in his understanding

179

of the priority of class struggle and a politics based on the "non-recognition" of any other form of social inequality as "authentic".) However, perhaps the faith in the existence of an "authentic class," or of an "authentic community" (a fraternity of comrades, or brothers and sisters in Christ), who can rightfully claim the name of the universal, should yet again be placed into question. The notion of an authentic community or people bears the special status of a secular myth of modernity, one that was born alongside the more archaic myths of nation and race, which are like its shadows and populist forms. But again, Levinas's critique of the "authentic form" of this collectivity that can only be found in the solitary subject may have a renewed value for us today. Does not this "I-you" collectivity return again in the political dyad of the friend-enemy couple, which continues to un-found any potential universalism of the collectivity of the "we?"

Returning now to our contemporary moment and to Badiou, his most explicit criticism comes in *Ethics*, written several years before the work on St. Paul, where he states: "To put it crudely: Levinas's enterprise serves to remind us, with extraordinary insistence, that every effort to turn ethics into the principle of thought and action is essentially religious."[27] Here, we are given a stark alternative between religious ethics and militant philosophy, which in some ways recalls Heidegger's somewhat "fundamentalist" viewpoint concerning the absolute hostility between faith and reason. As for Badiou, I suspect that it is the apparent success of Levinas's ethical principle of turning thought into a virulent form of active differentiation that poses the greatest problem for his own position of "anti-philosophy": how to combine the principle of thought and action in a pure element of Saying that is not merely determined as the introduction of another subjective production of difference in the worldly proliferation of alterities. As he discovers in "the unprecedented gesture" of St. Paul, it is only by laying claim to the position of the universal itself, and casting off all forms of relative difference, that this principle can be attained. Or, as he resolves a few years later in the conclusion of *Saint Paul*:

> This is why, as Paul testifies in exemplary fashion, universalism, which is an absolute (nonrelative) subjective production, indistinguishes saying and doing, thought and power. *Thought becomes universal only in addressing itself to all others, and it effectuates itself as power through this address.* But the moment all, including the solitary militant, are counted according to the universal, it follows that what takes place is the subsumption of the Other to the Same ... *The production of equality and the casting off, in thought, of differences are the material signs of the universal.*[28]

To conclude with a brief commentary on this passage, I don't think we can immediately accept this final claim that the cancellation of all differences that is first proposed in thought would be, in itself, sufficient to produce the material signs of equality among all others. (This is simply the hypostasis of thought and action.) More critical, however, is the claim that thought can address itself to all others, thereby "effectuating itself as power through this address." In fact, only Christian universalism could allow us to imagine such a thought, the unprecedented gesture of addressing "all of Humanity" – but in order to "effectuate itself as power through this address," it first of all needed the "concrete apparatus" (*dispositive*) that the Roman Empire later provided – something, by the way, that could never have been imagined by Paul in his own time, but which permanently remains as a precedent for our own.

Notes

A previous version of this statement appeared as "The Unprecedented Return of St. Paul," in Rosi Braidotti et al. (eds), *Post-Secular Publics: Transformations of Religion and the Public Sphere* (London: Palgrave, 2014).

1 Heidegger, *Pathmarks*, p. 41.
2 "This peculiar relationship does not exclude but includes the fact that *faith*, as a specific possibility of existence, is in its innermost core the mortal enemy [*todfeind*] of the *form of existence* that is an essential part of *philosophy* and that is factically ever-changing" (Ibid., p. 53).
3 Badiou, *Ethics*, pp. 20ff.
4 Badiou, *Saint Paul*, p. 5.
5 Ibid.
6 "In this regard, it is to its element of fabulation [*point de fable* – although I prefer to translate this phrase according to the Latin sense of *fabula* as form of "saying"] alone that Paul reduces the Christian narrative, with the strength of one who knows that in holding fast to this point as real, one is unburdened of all the imaginary that surrounds it" (Ibid., p. 5).
7 Ibid.
8 Ibid., p. 15.
9 Meeks, *The First Urban Christians*, p. 180 (emphasis mine).
10 Ibid., p. 180.
11 Badiou, *Saint Paul*, p. 37.
12 Ibid., p. 57. "Paul declared that for gentile Christians now to wish to be 'under the Law' would not be a step forward but backward, equivalent to a return to Paganism (Gal. 4:8–11). It would not be an act of obedience to God's will, but of disobedience toward the new order established by the Messiah's coming and crucifixion" (Meeks, *The First Urban Christians*, p. 176).
13 Badiou, *Saint Paul*, pp. 57–8 (emphasis mine).
14 Meeks, *The First Urban Christians*, p. 176.
15 Badiou, *Saint Paul*, p. 99.
16 Ibid., p. 109.
17 Ibid., p. 111.
18 Ibid., p. 57 (emphasis mine).
19 Badiou, *Ethics*, p. 20. Although, in the very same breath, Badiou will also admit that the popular conception of "the ethics of difference" does not fit with Levinas's "actual conception of things."

20 Ibid.

21 Levinas, *Existence and Existents*, p. 95.

22 Ibid., pp. 93–94.

23 Levinas, *Humanisme de l'autre homme*, pp. 80–1.

24 Levinas, *Existence and Existents*, p. 94.

25 Ibid., p. 95.

26 Ibid.

27 Badiou, *Ethics*, p. 23.

28 Badiou, *Saint Paul*, p. 109 (emphasis mine).

8

The Coming Community?

Finally, I now return to address the theme of "community" (including the literary and philosophical form of "negative community") that appears frequently in Nancy's writings throughout the 1980s. Here, I am specifically referring to the writings collected in *La Communauté désoeuvrée* (1986), which take as their overt subject a conception of community that is found in the pre-war writings of Georges Bataille, the French sociologist, philosopher, bibliophile, and co-founder of the *Collège de Sociologie* between 1937 and 1939. In *La Communauté affrontée* (2001), Nancy himself describes this period of his work as having begun in 1983 with the publication of the original essay version of "La Communauté désoeuvrée" in a special issue of *Aléa* around the themes of the "community" and the "number" (i.e., the mass, the crowd, but also addressing the new political concepts of the assemblage, the multiplicity, and the multitude). As he recounts, the return to Bataille's concept of community and particularly to the early writings on the "sacred sociology" and the "absence of myth" was an effort "to discover another possible resource for the concept of the political."[1]

Before this moment, Nancy writes, "community was a word that was ignored in the discourse of thinking."[2] In other words, philosophical discussions of the concept of community were infrequent and mostly took place in the public press around the formation of the European Union, especially with the passing of the Single European Act in 1986. Moreover, from the immediate post-war period through to the end of the Cold War, the Left had maintained an allergic reaction to any mention of this theme, given its historical association with the German *Volksgemeinschaft*. (For example, Nancy reports that the 1988 German translation of *La Communauté désoeuvrée* was labeled "Nazi" by a leftist journal in Berlin.) However, as Nancy also notes, over the next ten years, following the dissolution of the Soviet Union in 1991, a sudden and dramatic shift in the polarity of the concept's meaning occurred, as a result of which the term gradually becomes associated with the "return of/to communism" in France and Italy, in the writings of Agamben and Esposito, and, in the United States, with the publication of Hardt and Negri's *Empire* in 2000, marking the positive aspirations of the multitude and a new "communitarian" discourse.

By tracing a line through these three decades – the 1930s, the 1980s, and the 1990s, leading up to the current moment – I am highlighting a certain return of and to the theme of "community" in each historical moment, a theme that in each case either privileges, on the one hand, the communist community and communism, or, on the other, a quasi-religious secondary community or "community of affect" (*Bund*) as primary sociological notions. Perhaps, then, these multiple returns *of* and *to* "community" may allow for a more accurate determination of the underlying issue at stake in what is often and, in my view, mistakenly referred to as "the return of religion" in Western philosophy.[3] Taking account of all these transformations over a brief twenty-year period, Nancy himself summarizes the different

185

and even opposite meanings that are ascribed to the concept as the expression, symptomatically, of a more fundamental problem confronted by modern leftist political theory in general: Namely, the impossibility of founding the concept of the political on an actual instance of community; more precisely, the problem of establishing the rights of a particular expression of community on the basis of a politics that is assumed *a priori* to be truthful and just.[4]

In Bataille's own sociological research from the 1930s, the anthropological and religious notions of the sacred and sacrifice are explored to raise the possibility of an "abandonment" of the form of individuality to the group (as an act of donation, or as a gift) in a manner that is fundamentally different from the idea of the "substitution" of individual identity for the identity of the leader in modern fascism, or the negation of individual particularity for the collective identity according to the communist ideal. Nevertheless, even though Bataille's notion of community is offered as a critical rejection of the sociological principles belonging to the formations of fascism and communism in his time, he essentially retains the essential problem of community that lies at the basis of each political form.[5] Perhaps the immediate distinction we might make concerning the return to these themes in the 1980s is that in the post-war societies of France and Germany, and especially for a younger generation of intellectuals, any discussion of the sacred would immediately evoke an association with the community of fascism, and would thus simply be "unthinkable" in all the senses that term implies – unless, that is, it was presented in the form of a "negative community," as in the case of Nancy's writings. As for the idea of communism, in addition to assuming a more progressive and discursive form as "communitarianism," as already mentioned above with regard to the works of Hardt and Negri, it has either evolved into a utopian expression of "the coming community" (Agamben) – that is, into yet another expression of negative community, if not simply negative theology in Agamben's case – or, in the case of Badiou's "return to communism," into a more millenarian and "post-leftist" expression of "elective community" (i.e., "elective fidelity to the event") that in some ways recalls the motives behind Bataille's own communitarian projects in the 1930s. In this regard, we might recall the epigraph from the first issue of *Acéphale*, which appeared in 1936, taken from Kierkegaard's comment on the revolution of 1848: "What looks like politics and imagines itself to be politics, will one day reveal itself to be a religious movement."[6]

Finally, a third development that appears specifically in Nancy's resuscitation of Bataille's writings during the 1980s (which will be the primary focus of my reading) is the manner in which Nancy sometimes reduces some of the excesses that belonged to Bataille's original themes of community and the sacred (including ecstatic and intoxicated states of ritual experience) to the more "literary" forms of depersonalization and subjective abandonment that will determine the experience of "literature" – or "writing" (*l'écriture*) – that is, if we adopt, as Nancy suggests, "the acceptation of this word [today] that coincides with literature."[7] Here we find the basis for Nancy's proposal of a "literary communism," one in which neither "communism" nor "literature" should be understood in their habitual linguistic or overtly ideological senses, since it would not necessarily assume the form of a community of letters, but rather refers to a community that constitutes its understanding of "being-in-common" through the experience of writing and "the communication of works." This "coincidence" that Nancy inscribes into the concept of community will be the subject of my interrogation of the subjacent concepts of "literature, or writing" from this period, especially given that this emphasis on literary community contradicts in some important ways Bataille's own view of the revolutionary possibilities that belonged to the literary movements of his own time (e.g., "the Surrealist community"). This is why I have chosen to highlight Bataille's earlier reproach in the form of a question: Can "literature" (or "writing" today) again "assume the task of directing collective necessity?"[8]

After this all too cursory summary of the history behind the term "community," let us first return to Bataille's original notion of community from the pre-war writings. Being somewhat distinct from "society" or "the social," the notion of "community" for Bataille always refers to something mythical, that is, the expression of the sacred as the implicit presupposition of every social form. According to Bataille's original thesis of "the absence of myth," there are societies, including our present one, where a subject (an individual, a collective), *can* exist without community, or where the necessity of the sacred as the most intense expression of "being-in-common" is discovered to be absent, lost, destroyed, or simply forgotten through the historical processes of colonialism, modernization, or globalization. Following Bataille, in *La Communauté désoeuvrée* Nancy calls this a time of "myth interrupted," where the very mythic sense of community is suspended between two times, so to speak: between the "no longer," referring to what was formerly determined by ritual, and the "not yet" of the "community to come" which can (and in some ways cannot) simply be understood as the anticipation of a new mythic foundation of the social bond. The question I will return to below concerns the presumption of myth itself as a form of necessity for the idea of community.

Nevertheless, Bataille also claims that the time of a society that exists in the absence of myth (i.e., the absence of community) is itself a modern myth, if not the myth of modernity itself. In other words, this is *our myth today*, and we are present to it in the sense that we live in a time without origin, a time that is founded on nothing *other* than its own present, which is to say, a present without before or after, without order, which causes us to become dizzy and disoriented, ecstatic in our horizons, beside ourselves in the very moment. This dizziness, vertigo, or disorientation also defines our *passion* and our *passivity* before every other singular being with whom we share the present in the form of an essential absence of relation. It is as if every social relation is struck by this dizziness, brought about by its absence. In other words, according to the foundational principle of capitalist societies like our own, *no social relation is absolutely necessary*! Neither family nor kinship ties, blood or racial membership, class or social caste can any longer be said – that is, in an absolute sense that constitutes a general case of collective identity – to determine the location and ultimate destination of each singular being in its relation to others.

In the early writings on what he called "the Surrealist religion" Bataille focuses on the possibilities of the *Bund*, as a social organization or secondary community, in his list of collective forms that appear in modern post-industrial societies, marking an essential antagonism between what he called, following the sociological research of Jules Monnerot, the "community of fact" (race, nation, language) and the "community of affect" (the sympathetic or elective community):

The belonging of fact cannot satisfy us, since it does not allow our relation to others to be founded upon what is, according to the choice we make, most important for us. We are complete only outside ourselves, in the human plenitude of assembly, but we become complete only if, as we gather together, we do so in a way that responds to our most intimate demands. To the extent we no longer want to become ridiculous or disfigured in our own eyes [i.e., incomplete, solitary beings apart from community] we are in search of a secondary community whose aims are in complete accord with our own intimate being.[9]

Bataille calls this desire for secondary community, not without irony, our "sociological tendency."[10] In explaining this tendency he emphasizes the social organization of the *Bund* as a peculiar quasi-religious form of community and as the expression of a sociological tendency that will become a constant and ever-increasing feature of modern societies. As he writes:

It may even be that the consciousness of this radical difference, to which we are brought by more and more rapid subversions in the forms of social life, may introduce a new possibility into history: possibly people will finally realize clearly that there is no internal debate so profound that the historical movement of human societies cannot give it a *meaning*, and recognize at the same time that the *meaning* of this movement is not exhausted unless it is taken to the source of its intimate echoes.[11]

In the case of the Surrealist movement, which is a prototype of the "literary commune," it is a secondary community that is marked by its subversive characteristics and by the expression of the heterogeneity of its "being-in-common" in opposition to that of the surrounding society (*Gesellschaft*) to which it belongs. What distinguishes the space of this secondary community from society is the fact that – radically differentiating itself from the public, which is formed by the interactions of similar individuals – its members form a *finite whole* (a set within a set) that is heterogeneous with the surrounding social space and values. As Bataille writes, "it is a whole limited by individuals forming a whole that is different from a crowd."[12] Consequently, the particular subversive character of the avant-gardes from Surrealism onward can be sociologically explained by the creation of heterogeneous and "non-exchangeable" values that exist in relation to the larger society, which is governed by the principle of exchange. Nevertheless, its initial formation simply represents the sociological principle of the *Bund*, which is also found in most historical religions as well, and thus its expression contains the presumption that the unique values of the community are heterogeneous, or even posed as transcendent, to the larger society. Thus, in the case of the Surrealists who are the object of Bataille's earlier reflections, it is the expression of collective revolt against the "community of fact" and its affective community manifested in the creation of new values that will constitute the reversal of everything that the larger society has cast away (e.g., dreams, mystic trances, drugs), and specifically by a mode of communication that is determined as completely useless as information or work – namely, *literature*.

Here, we might understand the modern notion of "negative community" as a sociological form of *Bund* that actually precedes the various literary and philosophical movements that will institutionalize it as a dominant and partly mythic vehicle of culture, which is partly responsible for its generic determination associated with "the ideal community of literary communication" from Romanticism up to and even including the various expressions of communitarian discourses and literary communisms that belong to the present moment. Of course, Nancy writes:

191

This can always make for one more myth, a new myth, and not even as new as some would believe: the myth of the literary community was outlined for the first time (although in reality it was probably not the first time) by the Jena romantics, and it has filtered down to us through everything resembling the idea of "a republic of artists" or, again, the idea of communism (of a certain kind of Maoism, for example) and revolution inherent, *tels quels*, in writing itself.[13]

For Nancy, however, the word *literature* designates the very possibility that enters into our epoch; it is employed as an act of incision (or interruption) that constitutes the very scene of myth today, but in the same stroke erases the very traces of writing by means of which it has cut into its own myth.[14] If one excuses the overtly Derridean tones of this definition (although these overtones are everywhere in Nancy's own exposition), "literature" can be grasped as both the scene and the event of a double *ex-cision* of the foundational myth of society. It is an act of literature (that is to say, writing) that must first cut into all previous myths of community, and then in a second incision (which is actually an *ex-cision*) manages to cut away any traces of its own mythic performance, even performativity, as the scene of a modern myth. In other words, after the second stroke, the sense of this event no longer appears as literature (as writing), but rather as a new foundation for the experience of community itself, which accounts for the nature of its presentation as an interruption and suspension or deferment of the relations that compose actual existing society. Is this experience, then, merely a fiction in the negative sense of an essential deception or alibi? No. Because in wiping away all its own traces as writing it no longer appears as a fiction, and thus cannot be determined merely as a metaphor of lived experience, nor as its abstract or imaginary representative as in most common interpretations of ideology. Writing *is* lived experience, but an experience that is first of all founded upon an aporia. To cite a passage from Blanchot to which I shall return below, writing is "the sharing of 'something'" that seems always already to have eluded the possibility of being considered as a part of the sharing: speech, silence.[15] It is this *aporia* that will concern Nancy (and Blanchot, in a different manner, as we will see below) in a sense that it would not for Bataille, who saw the "literary community" as only one possibility of the *Bund* – and not even the most privileged expression of this "sociological tendency" – since, for him, modern cults and other secondary communities of culture and identity are too multiple to be reduced to one sociological principle of collective experience.

In order to illustrate this last point, let us return to Nancy's own definition of "community." He writes, "community means, in some way, the presence of a being together whose immanence is impossible except as its death-work."[16] Here, Nancy is not simply referring to the subjective and psychological states of mourning, nor even to the existential state of solitude and "being towards one's own death" (*Dasein*), but rather to the collective and ritual work of mourning as the performative and social character of speech and silence that this work enacts "in common" (*Mitsein*). Thus, this experience of community can only be present in the act of mourning as the presence of being together. We might ask, however, what is it that presences itself in a work of mourning that names a kind of being together that is not possible in any other social relation or possible mode of being together? This would presuppose that the being together of family or ethnic belonging would not encompass or approach this presence, nor the being together of a social project, or even of any type of activity including political activity.

What is it that is present in the being together of mourning, that is, *necessarily*, which may or may not be present in these other modes of being together? Nancy immediately reveals this exceptional trait as "the Word" (which remains capitalized in his own discourse). In the work of mourning the Word still retains a living relation to one who, by dying, is absented from every other form of belonging, and it is only through "the Word" that our being together is still preserved, even as a form of intimacy. As he writes elsewhere: "But in point of fact *désoeuvrement* itself cannot be understood otherwise than by starting out with the resurrection of death, if, by means of *oeuvre,* 'the word gives voice to death's intimacy.'"[17] In "a Word," our being together transcends death, but in a manner of immanence (or intimacy) that cannot be achieved within any other social relationship (i.e., neither in sexuality, nor work, nor in politics, etc.); therefore, in turn, this mode of presence, or of being together, exposes every other social relationship to its own constitutive limit, to an essential experience of its finitude or impossible coming to presence as a community. Therefore, as in the case of mourning, the work of *désoeuvrement* affected by "literature, or writing" (Nancy) suddenly appears to transcend every other social form of community, as if constituting the sovereign limit of every other manner of *being-in-common*.

Following Nancy's argument, at this point we might ask whether or not all writing is in some sense founded in mourning-work. In fact, we must allow this as a possibility. However, accepting this hypothesis, we must also allow the possibility that this represents a fundamental bias that belongs to Christianity, with the establishment of a *necessary* relationship between the presence of the Word and the presence of community that is encrypted within writing. Moreover, not only must we allow for the possibility that this relationship between "*the* Word" and "*the* Community" is a bias inscribed in the Christianized West, but also recognize it as an alibi or diversion invented by a particular notion of community that absolutely refuses the death of the individual and thus the loss of the demand of community itself – a demand for presence that exceeds even the biological death of its individual members! In other words, this is the danger specific to the transcendence of "the Word." Is the still current bias toward literature as a privileged site of collective experience something that precedes us, as Nancy says, "from the very depths of community"? And yet, in asking "what community?," or rather "where is community?," we find ourselves before a tautology, that is, before a mythological statement concerning origins, since the original community is precisely what is lacking, and it is this absence of community that is now only present in the form of a myth that belongs to writing itself, that is to say, to our *graphocentrism* today.[18]

Let us now return to Bataille's original statement concerning the relationship between "literature" and collective existence: "Literature [or writing, that is, according to Nancy, if we accept the coincidence of these two terms] cannot assume the task of directing collective necessity." In taking up this statement again, I will now refer to an early commentary by Blanchot in *La Communauté Inavouable* (1983), which appeared in the same year as the earlier version of "La Communauté désoeuvrée" and was written partly in response to Nancy's text, and in another respect will represent what Nancy later calls its *désoeuvrement*.[19] It is the occasion of this extremely elliptical and secretive communication by Blanchot to Nancy – so secretive that Nancy himself confesses to not quite knowing what Blanchot was saying to him – concerning the earlier even more secretive relationship that existed between Blanchot and Bataille. Nancy writes: "I was immediately struck by the fact that Blanchot's reply was, at the same time, an echo and a resonance or replication, a reserve, and even in some sense a reproach. Nevertheless, I have never been able to completely clarify this reserve or reproach, neither in the text, for myself, nor in correspondence with Blanchot."[20]

Turning to Blanchot's text, therefore, let's rephrase once more Bataille's original statement in accordance with Blanchot's commentary: *Literature is insufficient to direct collective necessity for the idea, much less the actual existence, of community.* Thus, the word *insuffisance* is underlined throughout Blanchot's commentary in reference to Bataille's primary thesis concerning what he defines as the governing principle of community, as well as our "sociological tendency": *the principle of insufficiency.* According to Bataille, "there exists a principle of insufficiency at the root of each being … a being, insufficient as it is, does not attempt to associate itself with another being to make up a substance of integrity," but rather, from the awareness of its own insufficiency, needs the other in order to place its own being in question.[21] This might appear counter-intuitive at first glance, since we usually or habitually imagine that a being that perceives its own insufficiency will seek in another the basis for its own completion, "integrism" or "fusion" (Nancy). And yet, because "insufficiency cannot be derived from a model of sufficiency," what Bataille calls "our own intimate being" must already be encompassed (and preceded) by the presence of another, or by a plurality of others (not yet a community) whose presence "triggers a chain reaction in each singular being."[22] In other words, the principle of insufficiency is nothing other than the presence of others whose presence triggers this chain reaction in each separate individual and causes the idea of community to come into being, especially since "a being is alone or knows itself to be alone only when it is not."[23]

Turning now to Nancy's reading of the term "insufficiency," it is also equated with the experience of "literature" (for which, we also recall, there is no name that is yet sufficient). However, in his commentary on Nancy's text, Blanchot, somewhat anxiously, calls into question this analogy, even going so far as to refute Nancy's central thesis that the nature of the separation effected by the movement of writing could in any way express the principle of insufficiency that determines each singular being in relation to community. As he argues:

> It does not follow that the community is the simple putting in common, inside the limits of what it would propose for itself, of a shared will to be several [à plusieurs], albeit to do nothing, that is to say, to do nothing else than maintain the sharing of "something" which, precisely, seems always already to have eluded the possibility of being considered as a part of the sharing: speech, silence.[24]

The above passage contains an allusion to the phrases that appear throughout Nancy's arguments concerning what has eluded the part of the sharing (part à un partage): speech, silence. How so? First of all, the material and psychological partitions that determine the speech and silence are not "parts" of our experience (Erfahrung) of being-in-common, but already attest to the fact of our separate and isolated existence as singular beings. As Bataille writes, "Communication is [already] ecstasy," the object of which is defined as "the negation of the isolated being."[25] Of course, Nancy also says that "communication is the constitutive fact of an exposition to the outside that defines singularity," but Blanchot calls into question whether this exposition can be identified with "the simple putting in common, [i.e., the act of writing], inside the limits of what it would propose for itself [i.e., a work, a text], of a shared will to be several [à plusieurs]."[26] Therefore, to say that writing is the privileged form of communication in which finitude appears (in "com-parution," Nancy says at this point) would simply risk producing yet another hypostasis of the Being of beings, or in Nancy's own words, *the presentation of a "primordial structure," at once "detached, distinguished, and communitarian."*[27]

Our question will concern, therefore, whether writing alone is "sufficient" to trigger the chain reaction noted earlier. In other words, is "literature, or writing" sufficient to represent this principle of insufficiency? Of course, it is true that writing can also be determined as the effect of a chain reaction that expresses a principle of insufficiency in each singular being, causing this being to actively expose itself to the other or a plurality of others – for recognition, identity, affirmation, contestation, work. Otherwise, why would writing exist if it did not testify to the insufficiency of the individual being, even in relation to its own "singular being," and open in us a supplementary and necessary dimension to our social existence? Nevertheless, does this exigency for writing express the principle of insufficiency, or does writing merely express itself as an abstract and superficial effect of a more primary principle of insufficiency, or "prime mover"?

What is this "prime mover"? Earlier we described death as the event that calls forth or co-invokes a plurality of others to come into being *qua* community, but precisely in the finite number of those members whose presence actualizes the physical existence of a community. Writing, here, can only evoke this event *en absentia*, by memorializing it in the form of a simulacrum that

198

may very well produce a chain reaction of effects that exposes each singular being to a plurality of others, but is incapable of causing this plurality to come into presence as *a finite community*. Therefore, if "literature, or writing" is to function in any way as commanding or directive, then it must first be set within a concrete social relationship. For Blanchot, moreover, without any relation to a particular other (as in the case of his own friendship with Bataille, which he maintains as a "secret") or to a plurality of others who constitute the possibility of community (as in the many communities Bataille himself founded, even if only to see them all splinter and fall apart), writing itself can only function as a dead letter. It is according to this same argument that Blanchot will write in *L'Attente, l'oubli:* "We should understand then why it should be that speaking is worth more than writing. Speech bears within itself the fortuitous character which links the impact of chance to the game. It depends immediately on life, on the humours and the fatigues of life, and it welcomes them as its secret truth."[28] Put another way, more provocatively, only the excessive presence of the other is sufficient to represent a summoning *directive*, and only the other's absence *in particular*, and *qua particular*, causes the solitary individual to live on as if "beside himself" (excluding even the substitution of the ego's own death as a model for this original *ek-stasis*, thereby fundamentally calling into question Heidegger's conception of *Dasein*). Bataille: "this is what puts me beside myself, *this is the only separation that can open me*, in its very impossibility, to the Openness of community."[29] Blanchot: "That is what founds community. There could not be a community without the sharing of that first and last event which in everyone ceases to be able to be just that (birth, death)."[30]

In the above passages, I have underscored Bataille's and Blanchot's arguments concerning the intimate relation between the death of the other (*qua* particular) and the finite principle of community because here we are confronted with the most glaring contradiction in their exposition of these themes: if being present to another "who absents himself by dying," even holding the hand of "another who dies," is the *only* decisive event of separation that opens the individual to community, then the actual condition of community would be necessarily finite, that is to say, un-sharable apart from those who experience it directly, and thus no principle could be drawn from this "limit-experience" to communicate this condition of being-in-common to others. Once again, this would appear to be counter-intuitive: how can the principle of community, which is normally understood to express the general or universal condition of *being-in-common* (*Mitsein*), be founded upon an event that is, by definition, in-communicable and un-sharable outside of those few who have experienced it, as if endowing its principle with an air of mystery and esoteric knowledge, and certainly exposing it to a certain religious signification?

And yet, we might ask, why would the death of the other, even in only referring to a particular other, and to the most common and insignificant death, be any less remote or mythical as a foundation for the idea of community than the death of a hero or a God?[31] In other words, the death of the other is the only event that separates me from myself, as an isolated being; that places the supposed self-sufficiency of my ego or my autonomy as a subject most radically in question. However, this death must be particular if it is to function as a summons of my separate existence, no longer as an isolated being, but as a being who is fundamentally dependent on the other, that is, a social being. This is why, ultimately, my own death cannot serve as a model, which would simply reaffirm my self-sufficiency and my autonomy, or my independence before others – even an indifference before the other's death, as if every other being were only a stranger and the ego remained locked in its own immanence. Moreover, if the only directive of collective existence is the death of a particular other – an other who, according to Bataille, must be "elected" from a plurality of others and whose social relation is not determined on the basis of a "community of fact" – then this is why the subject is always called to become part of a particular community, a finite community whose members "have a share" in death (always the death of a particular) as the condition of their being-in-common, even in those cases where a community can number no more than two members, as in a community of lovers (which is the title of the second part of Blanchot's response). In other words, because community is always finite, and can even be composed only of a few, it cannot become a permanent foundation of the whole, but always remains partial and incomplete, which is to say, a secondary whole.

There are many dangers to this kind of formulation – too many to recount in the space of this analysis. First of all, it limits the possibilities of community solely to the relation between individuals and would not seem to allow for a general principle of society that could include populations, and most importantly, strangers and those social others with whom the subject has nothing in common – in short, a relation of and between multiplicities or the "multitude." Nevertheless, this is the "sociological tendency" that we have already established at the basis of the *Bund*, the secondary community or the "community of affect" which is defined as "a whole limited by individuals forming a whole that is different from a mass or crowd."[32] If we were to concede to this principle, however, then we must also acknowledge that the concept of community be *completely insufficient* as the directive principle of any political project that seeks to organize the masses, the crowd, the multitude, as well as any democratic presentation of an assemblage of individuals (e.g., "We the people…"). In other words, there can be no "politics of community," because the historical community – determined as a secondary whole that is differentiated from a multiplicity – is formed either in retreat from the society that excludes it (as if constituting "a line of flight," or a "becoming minor"), or, as in the example of the Nazi community (*Volksgemeinschaft*), because the community totalizes the field of the political and thus excludes all politics. Certainly, this leads to a critique of the collective politics of fascism and racism, as exemplified in Bataille's own early analysis, but it may also reveal a fundamental dehiscence between the modern concepts of community and politics. In other words, as Nancy first observed, today there is the presence of a generalized "decoupling" of politics (i.e., sovereignty) from the experience of community (i.e., intimacy), and as a result both aspects have seemed to withdraw to a limit that cannot be totalized or assembled into one form. Although this may be good news with regard to the threat of a return of totalitarianism (which we now understand to belong to a historical moment of modernization), it exposes us to the idea of a multiplicity of politics without any common horizon, project, or universal genus – and thus, to a politics based purely on calculation and strategy.

At the same time, modern expressions of community could only have emerged alongside the equally modern notions of the masses or the crowd. As Blanchot writes, "theoretically and historically there are only communities of small numbers," and this fact exposes the principle of community to two dangers that are both quantitative in nature.[33] First of all, it exposes the social body of community to the problem of finitude in a way that is not possible for the masses or the crowd, either in the form of the loss of individual members who are too few in number, or in the equal danger of a fusion of large numbers into the form of a supra-individual (the nation, the race) that exposes the group to possibilities of collective death, or genocide, or, more recently, nuclear extermination. For Bataille, "the tendency to fusion" only intensifies the presence of death for each individual, and the society that is composed or fuses itself into an aggrandized identification exposes every member of society to the same death (e.g., the death of Christ, the death of Hitler, etc.). As Blanchot writes, this "tendency towards a *communion* ... is ... an effervescence assembling the elements only to give rise to a unity (a supra-individuality) that would expose itself to the same objections arising from the simple consideration of the individual, locked in its own immanence."[34]

Again, let us recall the almost physical description of finitude as "a chain reaction" that the existence of the other or a plurality of others effects in the existence of every singular being, but in the form of a community that must be maintained in a high degree of tension, which Bataille earlier equates with conscious-ness brought about by the death of another. If this chain reaction that Blanchot speaks of becomes indeterminate and trails off into the realm of higher quantities, it would "risk losing itself in infinity," or splintering apart "just as the universe composes itself only by unlimiting itself in an infinity of universes."[35] According to Bataille, the only way for a community to persist in being is for it to maintain itself in the consciousness of death and to manifest this presence to its highest degree of tension within each of its members, as if to constantly re-invoke death's directive as a foundation of the *Bund*. It is also around this commanding directive that we find Bataille's interest in the ritual forms of sacrifice in many primitive religions, but also the basis for his critique of these forms as well as of the sociology of fascism as precisely a resistance to the truth of community itself: precisely its temporal finitude and its smaller quantities.

In the later writings from the period of the *Collège de Sociologie*, for example, there is a constant relationship demonstrated between the sociological form of fascism as a "mass phenomenon" and the necessity of war as the most prevalent means of manifesting the immanent presence of death, at its highest degree of intensity, within each singular being as a power "sufficient" to co-invoke the absolute directive of the fascist community. In this case, the group binds itself to the myth of community and consequently negates the entire principle of the number in favor of a fusional principle of identity, modeling itself in some ways after a community of souls, or a community of lovers, which only require a number of $N + 1$. Community, being founded on a principle of homogeneity, is constitutionally opposed to the heterogeneity of the number or the multiplicity, especially to any heterogeneity among its own numbers, however few.

It is around this phenomenon, finally, that we also discover that the same principles of finitude and number will also be responsible for the greatest threat of all: the loss of community itself in the death of all its members (at once), thereby ruining the habitual possibilities of immanence and transcendence for both the individual and the group. Here we find the form of *communion* that threatens to become a principle of sufficiency for community, and which Nancy often evokes as the explicit threat of a "fusional fulfillment in some collective hypostasis."[36] Among the instances of this kind of "fusion," of which the Christian

Eucharist is given as a primary symbol, Blanchot invokes the contemporary example attested to by "the sinister collective suicide in Guyana."[37] The fact that the Jones community of Guyana made the symbolic meaning contained in the Eucharist a literal expression of the sharing of death by each of its members, almost as a grotesque parody of the "Last Supper," ruins the possibilities of both immanence and transcendence for both the individual and the community.

How is immanence and transcendence ruined? If the immanence of community can only exist as a conscious idea of the death of the other which "interrupts" the separate and isolated existence of the ego, then the death of every particular (at once, in the act of collective suicide) would negate both the space of consciousness and the necessity of community. In short, if everyone dies, then community is no longer necessary, and exists from that moment much in the same way ruins exist: as only the traces of a now extinct society. At the same time, what Blanchot refers to as the "habitual forms of transcendence" – meaning that there is more than one form – are ruined by the fact that it is precisely the death of the other as a particular (i.e., as a separate and isolated being) that makes it possible for a community to transcend this event by sharing this separation among all the others. Thus, the consciousness of community is extinguished only in the position of its separate existence in the individual, but undergoes redistribution among the survivors for whom the presence of others still causes a chain reaction that interrupts the separate and isolated existence. In the case of the collective suicide, however, transcendence is ruined, meaning that it is no longer necessary since no one survives and the spark that ignites the initial chain reaction is also extinguished, like trying to light a match underwater. Therefore, if the consciousness of

205

community is only immanent in the death of each particular, and at the same time transcendent in its separation from the death of every particular, then the "fusion" of the death of the particular and the collective in one gruesome act of collective suicide becomes the highest expression of a model of sufficiency that haunts every finite community.

Returning to Nancy, it is not by accident that we find again the term "fusion" to represent the greatest threat, or that writing is offered up as our only possible defense. In other words, it is only writing that makes possible the idea of communication "without a bond *and* without communion, equally distant from any notion of connection or joining from the outside and from any notion of a common and fusional interiority."[38] This formulation is everywhere present throughout Nancy's work, even constituting a major "philosopheme" (as Derrida would also say in *Le Toucher*), in the sense that we could find in all his writings one theme that is stated repeatedly: *communication without the threat of communion, outside any common identity, or danger of fusional interiority*. In view of this dangerous and threatening horizon, perhaps the highest task of his philosophy is precisely to expose every living community to this limit, thereby making it unworkable; to de-mythologize all presumptions of community based on the presence of a "common being," that is, at the very moment when any collective threatens to convert its own substance into the epiphany of community – to effect a "revelation" of the singular plurality of "being-in-common."[39] It is in this sense that we might understand Nancy's concept of community as negative, but not in the usual senses accorded to this notion, which correspond to *the Bund*, or the secondary community. For Nancy, the negative is purely procedural or poetic, the manner in which he occupies the theme of community only to unwork it, to untie it from every social bond and every possible communion, even though he will later acknowledge Blanchot's earlier criticism that this apotropaic gesture was perhaps too absolute in its negation of any "fusional intimacy" however brief and excessive, recalling that Bataille saw the collective experience of the *Bund* as a possibility of freedom from "the community of fact" (race, class, nation, language), or, today, one might also say "the community of the number" (whether this is understood as a political or as an economic formation of neoliberal society).

I conclude by returning to the genealogy of the theme of community as it appears in Nancy's most recent reflections since 2001. Here, it is important to note that Nancy employs the term "community" less frequently, preferring instead to concentrate his work around the less graceful term "with" (*avec*), as in "being-with" or "being-together," in place of "community" which now appears to him to bear a new set of risks in association with the re-emergence of fascist tendencies in European societies at the turn of the millennium, especially in France with the rise of Le Pen and the National Front in the elections that would take place just one year after Nancy published the following comments:

> In many respects I have come to understand the dangers posed by the use of the word community: its inevitable resonance with substance and a replete interiority, its just as inevitable Christian connotations (spiritual community, fraternal communion) or more broadly religious significations (Jewish community, community of prayer, community of believers), and its current usage, only applied it seems to so-called "ethnicities," could only caution us.[40]

Again, in the context of the mid-1980s, Nancy had simply attempted to find in the unpublished writings of Bataille conceptual resources around the theme of community that would escape the dangers of both fascism, on the one hand, and the coming neoliberal society, on the other. In this context, he took the risk of invoking the word community at that moment, even if it was only in an effort to abandon the myth of community by reducing it to a "common limit where singular beings share one another" (i.e., to "literature, or writing").[41] Twenty years later, however, it seems he had to return again to abandon the word itself in view of its various associations with the new communities of fascism, or in relation to the potential abuses and dangers evoked in the term "ethnic community," but most importantly, in view of the tendency of the current neoliberal society to immediately ruin whatever new chances a renewal of the concept of community could provide to our political discourse today. In some ways, this repeats a similar set of circumstances earlier experienced by Bataille and Blanchot during the immediate pre-war period concerning the concept of democracy, and may even indicate a new prohibition on the usage of the term community in current philosophical discourse, despite the promise of its association with new communitarian ideals, or with a "return of communism."[42]

Is the theme of "community" now running the risk of becoming, yet again, "excessive" and "inappropriate" as a *philosopheme* or as an element of our current political discourse? Is the "inappropriateness" of community something that is "proper to Man?"[43] Moreover, must the idea of "the return of community" (but also the "return of religion") always be destined to be associated with the dual horizons of fascism and communism, both of which are resolutely past, and yet, always still just over the horizon and yet to come – but always in a new sense that is both more promising and threatening at once? Is there not the possibility of another horizon, a third horizon, perhaps? In reply to these questions, I think Blanchot understood the problem best when he reminded us that the concepts of fascism and communism, even in their common usage in the 1980s, were in no manner equivalent and could not even be said to have the same meaning as the concepts employed in the 1930s. As he writes à propos "the premonition of what is already fascism," its "meaning ... as well as its becoming, eludes the concepts then in use, forcing thought to reduce it to what is common and miserable in it, or, on the contrary, pointing out what is important and surprising in it."[44] Of course, it is not surprising to hear implicitly the defense of a certain historical difference of the situation faced by European intellectuals in the pre-war period, or then again in the immediate post-war environment, especially given Blanchot's own personal history; but more importantly, we still find the admission of a certain "conceptual ambiguity" and a suspicion concerning the "abandonment" of both concepts to their most common or vulgar historical meanings. Concerning both dangers he sees lurking in the uses of the terms communism and community in Nancy's text, Blanchot simply observes that while "dishonored or betrayed concepts do not exist, concepts that are not appropriate without their proper-improper *abandonment* (which is not simple negation) ... do not permit us to calmly refuse or refute them."[45]

Notes

A previous version of this statement appeared as "Literary Communism," in Verena Conley and Irving Goh (eds), *Nancy Now* (London: Polity Press, 2014), pp. 37–58.

1 Nancy, *La Communauté affrontée*, pp. 31–2.

2 Ibid., p. 26.

3 Nevertheless, Nancy's own writings from the period I am referring to – particularly on community and "the community of those who have no community" – had a direct influence on the phenomena known as the "return to religion" in North American circles of continental philosophy. In an interview that appears in *Le Magazine littéraire* in 2003, Nancy describes the "return to religion" as a "new political correctness (and thus indecency)," referring specifically to its resurgence in academic philosophy in the United States, but also to the writings of Agamben, Esposito, and others.

4 Nancy, *La Communauté affrontée*, pp. 31–2.

5 For the sake of historical accuracy, it is important to note that democracy is not even entertained as a possibility, given the weakened and corrupt forms of Western democracies at precisely this moment. This is something that Nancy and Blanchot both underline in their more recent replies to various attacks on the writings from the pre-war years by Bataille, Blanchot, and other French intellectuals. See ibid., p. 16.

6 Quoted in Hollier, *Le Collège de Sociologie: 1937–1939*, pp. 55ff.

7 Here, we must note that Nancy never says "literature is writing," but rather, always, offers the alternative, "literature, or writing," that is, if we accept the "coincidence" of these two terms according to the modern invention of the myth of writing, but also with regard to the power accorded to this new myth to essentially "interrupt," if not to suspend, all the previous mythical foundations of community. Therefore, as Nancy writes, "a name we have given to this voice of interruption [of the myth of community]: literature (or writing, if we adopt the acceptation of this word that coincides with literature)." See Nancy, *The Inoperative Community*, p. 63.

8 Hollier, *College of Sociology*, p. xxvi. Specifically, the rejection of literature is a common denominator of the three texts that appear in the July issue of *La Nouvelle Revue* (1937), and especially in the collective manifesto of the College of Sociology initialed by Roger Callois, "For a College of Sociology." In "The Sorcerer's Apprentice," Bataille denounced artistic activity as a product of the dissociation of the complete man (*l'homme integral*). In a letter he had already told Kojève that the man of unemployed, purposeless negativity was unable to find in the work of art an answer to the question that he himself is.

9 Bataille, *Absence of Myth: Writings on Surrealism*, p. 109.

10 This is from a review of Monnerot's book, *Le faits socaux ne sont pas des*

choses (1946), that appears in the first issue of *Critique* (June 1946). This theme will be dominant in most of Bataille's writings in the immediate post-war period and follows from the research undertaken by the College of Sociology collective between 1937 and 1939, in which Monnerot was a member.

11 Bataille, *Absence of Myth: Writings on Surrealism*, p. 111.

12 Ibid.

13 Nancy, *The Inoperative Community*, p. 64.

14 Ibid., p. 72.

15 Blanchot, *The Inavowable Community*, p. 15.

16 Nancy, *The Inoperative Community*, p. 80.

17 Nancy, *Dis-enclosure: The Deconstruction of Christianity*, p. 90.

18 Although Nancy's own logic is sometimes quite tortuous around this question of origins, especially concerning the original myth of writing, I will only note here that he often uses the terms "myth" and "mythology" negatively, in the sense of lies or diversions, even while he speaks of a bias that precedes us unconsciously from "the very depths of community."

19 Nancy, *La Communauté affrontée*, p. 39.

20 Ibid., p. 38.

21 Blanchot, *The Inavowable Community*, p. 15.

22 Ibid., pp. 7–8.

23 Ibid., p. 5.

24 Ibid., p. 15.

25 Quoted in ibid., p. 18.

26 Ibid., p. 15; see also Nancy, *The Inoperative Community*, p. 29.

27 Nancy, *The Inoperative Community*, p. 29 (emphasis mine).

28 Blanchot, quoted in ffrench, *After Bataille: Sacrifice, Exposure, Community*, p. 132. For an alternative and, in many respects, parallel discussion of this episode, the reader should refer to chapter 3 of this excellent study of Bataille.

29 Quoted in Blanchot, *The Inavowable Community*, p. 9.

30 Ibid.

31 The Christian community, at least in its Pauline formulation, is established (or founded) on the death of Christ *qua* particular, and it is from this relationship that every Christian receives a new identity as "a brother or sister in Christ." Of course, this gives the Christian community an occult character, and the non-believer would never be able to fathom the deeply personal and real grief expressed by certain Christian communities, including many that exist today, in the ritual observance of the crucifixion.

32 Bataille, *Absence of Myth: Writings on Surrealism*, p. 111.

33 Blanchot, *The Inavowable Community*, p. 6.

34 Ibid., p. 7.

35 Ibid., p. 6.

36 Ibid., p. 7.

37 Ibid. What is commonly referred to as the "Guyana massacre" took place in 1978, five years before Blanchot's comments.

38 Nancy, *The Inoperative Community*, p. 29.

39 Ibid., p. 63. Upon invoking this word, Nancy interrupts himself in the voice of another as if to interrupt the invocation of a new myth, which would be a danger he also wants to avoid: "Certainly, there is a work only if there is a 'revelation' (you might interrupt me here: What are we to make of the use of this word 'revelation'? Does it not go along with 'myth,' as it does moreover with 'image'? But this is the space of absolute unsuitability: each one of these words also bespeaks its own interruption.)"

40 Nancy, *La Communauté affrontée*, p. 32.

41 Nancy, *The Inoperative Community*, p. 73. In this context it is important to recall that Lacoue-Labarthe, in the same moment and even in his collaboration with Nancy, never employed the concept of community or sought to give it any political use, since for him the term would always refer to the social environment of fascism. See Nancy, *La Communauté affrontée*, p. 32n.

42 In a 2011 interview with Philip Armstrong and Jason Smith, published as *Politique et au-delà*, Nancy expresses a similar anxiety concerning Alain Badiou's definition of politics as "destinée collective de l'humanité," which recalls a similar statement made by Napoleon to Goethe: "Le destin, c'est la politique." In reply to both statements, Nancy recalls the following line from a 1993 interview with Derrida: "Le 'politique' lui-même est un philosopheme – et finalement très obscure." Nancy, *Politique et au-delà*, pp. 50–2.

43 The theme of an excessive trait that is "proper to man" is properly Derrida's and concerns the following series covered in his last writings: sovereignty–stupidity–freedom. See Derrida, *The Beast and the Sovereign*, vol. 1.

44 Blanchot, *The Inavowable Community*, p. 5.

45 Ibid., pp. 1–2.

Conclusion: The Return Address

Life is no argument; error might be among the conditions of life. (Nietzsche, *The Gay Science*)[1]

In departing from the different subroutines of the past decade or so, and for the purposes of investigating a new "return address," which is "Life itself," I now turn to the last text that Foucault wrote shortly before his death in 1984, which is a revision of the preface he wrote earlier for the English translation of Canguilhem's *Le Normal et le Pathologique*, "La vie: L'experience et la science." Over the last ten years I have returned to reflect on this short preface often because I consider it, in some ways, as both a summary of Foucault's methodological trajectory – which, moreover, gives us some hint of the directions that his analytic might have taken if the HIV virus had not interrupted its course – and as a diagnosis of the inner logic of the function of the "return statement" in the contemporary field of philosophy during the same period.

Following Canguilhem's own understanding of the history of science, Foucault outlines the manner in which each philosophical epoch can be described in terms of the way it constitutes a composition of particular traits that can be found across the various positions and schools that might occupy each moment, the frequency and repetition of which establish a kind of equilibrium that is often mistaken for a historical continuum. In Foucault's own words:

> Philosophy can thus be defined as nothing more than the composition of particular traits in the period in which they appear, being the coherent figure, the systemization and the reflective form of their appearance; at the same time, each epoch appears as nothing other than the emergence and the manifestation of what in its essence is called philosophy – as an element that is more or less the revelation of significations belonging to that particular epoch.[2]

To apply this observation to our present context, let me underline the last statement: what is called philosophy (or "theory") is nothing other than the very "element" of epochal signification. However, for Foucault this "element" must be something *more* than mere signifying – as he claims, it is "irreducible" to a certain structure of language – and rather concerns the manner in which certain discursive practices simultaneously produce the objects about which they speak.[3]

In addition, here I might also recall a statement that appears midway through Bergson's *Introduction to Metaphysics*, where Bergson calls our attention to a certain "faculty" that appears beneath the diversity of analytical positions and divergent points of view, which he describes as something "simple and definite like a sounding of which one feels that it has more or less reached the bottom of a same ocean, even though it brings each time to the surface very different materials."[4] In a similar manner, the archeological image Foucault often employs for his own analysis of the discrete objects of what he calls discursive

214

practices (representation being only one practice among others) simply demonstrates the fact that the composition of traits one finds assembled across a particular period doesn't explain how these objects are articulated together in a system of thought or culture. Their only commonality is a quasi-temporal dimension, which doesn't itself appear as a container, but is simply related by being found to exist on the same level, or stratum. In *The Archaeology of Knowledge* (1969) we find that these significations are not – or no longer – defined as groupings of signs (i.e., signifying elements referring to contents of representations), and here we should recall that in this work, which followed *The Order of Things* (1966), Foucault was most concerned with distinguishing his conception of the element of signification from a synchronic series of elements belonging to language (*langue*).[5]

To illustrate Foucault's thesis concerning deeper epistemological arrangements, or Bergson's intuition of a simple, definite, and common "faculty" below the diversity of analytical propositions that belong to a particular moment, we can identify a "composition of particular traits" in a number of recent "return statements" in contemporary philosophy and theory: First, the theme of "Life itself" (immanent, sovereign, bare, disposable, etc.). Second, the emergence, manifestation, and revelation of a number of significations that have surfaced around Foucault's own concept of "biopower" in a manner that vividly recalls Bergson's metaphor that these are all soundings of the same ocean bottom. Third, the significations of new forms of biopolitical calculability in larger demographic, economic, and ecological terms that have transformed the current analysis of "politics" itself, which can no longer be simply oriented by the Aristotelian distinction of the "sovereign good" (*kuriōtatou*) of the individual, the community, or the *polis*, but rather is oriented

215

toward that "minimum of being" necessary to extend an earlier concept of sovereignty outward to enclose all other forms of life, including objects and inorganic matter. At the same time, it is also clear that what all these particular traits lack in the present context is what Foucault refers to above as "a coherent figure," or a systematization that provides a reflective form of appearance. In other words, what we lack is a simple and definite understanding of what Foucault calls the very element of signification today, whether this element is understood temporally, logically, or semiotically as the reflective form of a structure or system.

And yet, Life (or perhaps, "Life itself") cannot provide such an element, not only because its very condition is the power of error, whether according to a "vitalist" argument or according to modern genetic biology, but also because it remains and will always remain conceptually incoherent (i.e., unrationalizable), which is not the same as saying that it is irrational according to a moral argument. In an article entitled "The Concept of Life," published around the same time as Foucault's *Order of Things*, Canguilhem first observed that it is impossible to imagine the resolution of Life in the form (let us say, the frame) of a concept in the Kantian sense, since it would be necessary to speak of a multiplicity of conceptualizations (biological, chemical, neurological, but also ontological and moral–aesthetic – as in the conceptualization of the "good life" [*zoe agathon*]). Instead, Canguilhem employs the understanding of the purely logical and regulative function of the Idea from Kant's First Critique ("The appendix to the transcendental dialectic") to give the concept a transcendental function as signifying the "horizon" of a conceptual multiplicity (which Canguilhem calls a *territoire*), also recalling Foucault's own description of an epoch as a systematic reflection of a conceptual territory formed by particular traits.

Today, for example, this element can no longer be found in any language (*langue*), nor in the idea of structure itself, which formerly provided a reflective form of appearance for organizing these significations. Instead, and only very recently, power has become the element in which life first becomes an *expressive matter* that functions as an element of signification – perhaps in the same way that Bergson describes memory as "the spiritualization of matter" – except that this element does not assume the classical form of a table for classifying all the manners or degrees of life in its totality, since our present analysis is directed precisely toward those regions where life is composed of unformed matters, just as power has assumed the form of a purely virtual being that can only be reflected in other living bodies. Over the past forty years, research in genetics and genomics, the convergence of the latter with digital technology, and the intrusion of technology into all forms of life have called into question the idea that life is anything simple, natural or biological, and have made available knowledge and resources that may determine mutations or new aggregations in the constitutive elements of life forms and living systems, likely transforming the conditions of existence of life on the planet irreversibly.

Although there is no space to fully develop this point here, I would suggest that what we are witnessing today may have striking parallels with Foucault's own early observations concerning what he called the disappearance of language in the mid-point of the nineteenth century. Ironically, rather than constituting our advancement into these regions of being, we are witnessing the gradual "demotion" of the categories of both power and life as distinct objects of empirical knowledge, which have instead assumed a new metaphysical function in designating the enigmatic core of our being. Of course, here I am restricting

217

this function to how these categories are employed in philosophy (or "theory") today, rather than for example in the biological sciences, which in some respects might be compared to how the category of "language" functioned with the emergence of literature at the beginning of the twentieth century, according to Foucault's famous thesis from the conclusion of *The Order of Things*.

My concluding question, therefore, is whether we might conceive this epochal form of error in terms of what Bergson defined as a "faculty" that lies behind all the analyses it first sets into motion, and which emanates from a different source than the analytical faculty itself, which Bergson calls the retroactive effect, in the form of an error which vitiates our conception of the past, as well as our "pretension to anticipate the future for every occasion."[6] In each living occasion that the truth is posited in whatever system, error is assigned the position of the past by means of retrograde movement.[7] For Deleuze, this anticipatory pretension refers to the time-image, thus it could be said that the truth is nothing other than "a time-image" that belongs to the history of philosophy itself, which appears retroactively in the form of a possible future. Moreover, how does the form of error first emerge in thought except as an "act" that at first remains unconscious, but which in some cases evolves in order to traverse an entire field or period of thinking – that is, until it is actualized as a "coherent figure" of error that comes to define that period? In what way, we might ask, does this pattern of emergence and manifestation differ from the communication of anomalies in other systems, including organic and cybernetic systems?

In the "History of Mentalities," to employ an older term utilized by Cassirer and Maravall, it is usually in the form of polemics that the simple act of error virtual or latent within any system of human thought is gradually actualized in a manner that sometimes transforms the entire system of thought itself, or produces a system that becomes discontinuous with its own internal logic, and it is from this discontinuity that a new system emerges that in many ways transforms all the particular significations that composed the previous one. (For example, it is precisely at such moments that the same concept can suddenly acquire two completely contradictory or diametrically opposed meanings.) Here, I am not referring to the function of discontinuity that is often expressed by polemics within a given field, which occur continuously and belong to a distributive and reproductive logic, but to the general polemic that is often cast between different epochs, in which the regime of truth that emerges in one epoch serves as a "corrective" to the truth of a previous epoch, as when we refer to the Cartesian error of mind-body dualism, the Kantian error of the transcendental Subject, or today, to the errors of "correlationalism" or the Anthropocene. If we can summarize a general trend of philosophy and theory today, it would certainly be the return to a naïve scientific and atheistic notion of consciousness as a high-point of all phenomena, but this assumes that even in the absence of a subject (whether of language, or the psyche) consciousness can still exist on its own.[8] In most cases, it is not the existence of the Subject that is bracketed, according to the requirements of a radical *epoché*, but rather the reality of "the Other," or the socially symbolic world of others. As Lacan argued, a purely materialist conception of consciousness represents the constitution of the universe from a position of absolute narcissism, which Freud had already diagnosed as a symptom of science with its phantasy of imagining a universe without others, as a world of pure atoms outside or prior to the existence of the

Subject. In many respects, I would understand the most recent claims of speculative realism (based on a world without others) and object-oriented ontology (a world of objects without the Subject) to represent versions of a new scientific materialism or cosmology. However, even in a world of pure objects, the ego must be posited as the first, most primitive object relation; therefore, even in the radical act of bracketing consciousness of the Subject, there always remains a primitive and "pre-subjective" reflection of the ego itself, which appears like the famous image of the moon reflected in a prehistoric glacial lake (as in the case of the world of "the arche-fossil," for example).[9] As Lacan once said of similar materialist claims in his own time (the 1950s), "we should realize that everything that is properly speaking illusory isn't always subjective, [since] there are illusions that are perfectly objective, objectifiable, and it isn't necessary to make the whole of our distinguished company disappear for you to understand that."[10]

Returning to Foucault's exposition of Canguilhem, if error can be taken as the common name for what we might call, following Deleuze, our "dark precursor," then it is not a faculty that belongs specifically to Man – i.e., error is not, first of all, an "act" that is introduced by the presence of the Subject. On the contrary, if it can be nominally defined as an "act" at all, rather than a specific kind of event in a causal series, then its causal agency belongs to "life," as when Foucault says: "At the limit, life – and here in its most radical character – is that which alone is capable of error."[11] Therefore, as an aside, we might also pause to consider whether all the pretensions to bracket the Subject of an anthropomorphic frame will, in the end, be successful in rectifying the truth about our knowledge of the world of objects or the environment, since it is clear from Foucault's arguments that the factuality of error is not rooted in the experience of the Subject in its initial opening to the world, but rather in what he refers to here as "the errors of Life itself." The hallmark of Foucault's later philosophy, and its final point of divergence with phenomenology, is that he never bestowed upon the notion of Life any regulative function in the Kantian sense of an Idea of reason; consequently, we cannot even say that the idea of Life is a "transcendental illusion," but only that it is a category that has undergone quite sudden and discontinuous shifts, which, in turn, have successively transformed the nature of reason itself. The concept of life thus also has a history, but this does not have the same sense for Foucault as a "history of metaphysics" does for Heidegger.

In his own understanding of the concept of error, therefore, Foucault is no longer referring to the philosophy of Heidegger (who is perhaps, after Nietzsche, the greatest thinker of the history of the error called "truth"), but is rather referring to modern biological science and the manner in which the events of error occur in an evolutionary chain, usually through the expression of anomalies or mutations in genetic sequences. He writes:

> We must take into account how anomalies traverse the entire field of biology. It is also necessary to take account of mutations and the evolutionary factors that induce them. And equally it will be necessary to interrogate this singular albeit hereditary form of error, which comes from the fact that in the human life [or in Man] life achieves the form of a living being that is never found to be completely in its own place, a species-being that is fated "to err" and "to be deceived."[12]

If in the above passage we substitute the passive construction "to be mis-taken" for the active form of "to err," perhaps we might come closer to the essence of Foucault's thought: in "the form of man," life reaches the form of a living being that (1) deceives life; (2) is a singular form of life that is constituted by error; and (3) is a species whose fundamental distinction is that its own species-determination is bound up with the eventuality of the forms of error that determine the limits of this species. This last formulation would be Foucault's version of the Anthropocene. Here, one can easily point to the opposition of truth and falsehood as a universal trait defining human societies, including the values that different societies and different institutions have bound to this distinction. Following these observations concerning the different formations of error (chemical, biological, but also cybernetic) that will now need to be incorporated into the frame of philosophical representation in constructing any genealogical history of truth, Foucault makes perhaps the most striking claim that the entire history of philosophy can be understood as a discontinuous series of "corrections" to the radical capacity of life to "err" (but also to evolve through mutation, anomaly, and creative diversity), and the creative capacity of man to "be deceived" at each stage into thinking that this pertains to his powers as a subject. Consequently, if one admits the proposition that Life = the radical capacity to err, then one must also conclude that error is the root of what has also constituted the *moral (i.e., "human") value of truth* from the beginning, since it is in the struggle against the power of the error that the concept of truth assumes for each epoch "the dimension of what is proper to the life of human beings and thus is indispensable to the temporality of the species."[13]

Although Foucault's earlier application of the radical principle of discontinuity to describe epochal transformation was far too paradigmatic – and I would even say "prosaic" in a Hegelian sense – it is precisely corresponding to Canguilhem's insights during the same period concerning the concept of Life that he comes to a more precise thesis concerning the causality of these sudden revelations of new significations that determine each philosophical epoch. For example, from his archival research, Foucault observes that between 1520 and 1850 approximately 4,000 different pamphlets and articles appeared under the titles of "science of police in the broad sense" and "science of the police in the strict sense," and from this empirical evidence he deduces the concept of biopower to refer to this larger field of *Polizeiwissenschaft*, which gradually transforms the studies of economics, political science, public administration, medicine and philosophy.

In a very elliptical fashion, Foucault enunciates two other fundamental moments in this history: First, the Cartesian discovery concerning the relation of truth and the subject in the value of certainty. (Here, we might recall Descartes fable of the *Malin Genie* as the ultimate proof of the cogito's existence, but Foucault understands this figure more radically as a figure of Life itself, in which the certainty of the cogito would only be in the form of an essential "self-deception" that determines its history from that point onward.) Second, Foucault invokes two great texts that hail from the eighteenth and early nineteenth centuries: Kant's *Critique of Judgment* (on the critique of taste, or the science of true judgments) and Hegel's *Phenomenology of Spirit* (on the truth of the dialectic of reason which is capable of absorbing the power of error itself and converting it into a form of progress of the spirit of reason). These two works, according to Foucault, constitute the first grand philosophical formulations of the relation between truth and life – i.e., the first modern expressions of "bio-philosophy."

In conclusion, let me return to Foucault's reformulation of the concept of truth toward the end of his brief preface. He writes, "The creation of truth is only the most recent error, the decision concerning the true life in the most profound manner [is this not elsewhere defined as the essence of philosophy itself?], and the value accorded to the truth constitutes the most singular manner that life has invented, in the form of man, at the very point of its origin, carrying within itself the eventuality of error."[14] Here, on first glance, we might immediately note that this formulation is unusually metaphysical in the creative agency it assigns to life, which would be more consistent with the philosophies of Bergson or Deleuze than with Foucault's own earlier writings on the concept of life. In fact, this is the major statement that Deleuze takes up in the appendix to *Foucault* and recasts in the form of a metaphysical "dice-throw." As he writes: "the question that continually returns is therefore the following: if the forces within man compose a form only by entering into a relation with forms from the outside, with what new forms do they now risk entering into a relation, and what new form will emerge that is neither God nor Man?"[15] Concerning the unfolding of these epochal forms Deleuze immediately cautions us that it is necessary to speak tentatively of this eventuality without descending to the level of cartoons.[16]

Nevertheless, we find that it is also around this statement that Deleuze draws some remarkable and, at the same time, highly speculative conclusions concerning the potential regroupings of the forces of life and power in parallel with the earlier destination of literature that I mentioned above. Accordingly, the forms of error that are expressed by molecular biology and third-generation machines are defined in terms of modern literature, which "uncovers a 'strange language within language' and, through an unlimited number of superimposed grammatical constructions, tends towards an atypical form of expression that marks the end of language as such."[17] In other words, the forms of error employed by the forces of life and labor (i.e., power) bear more than a passing resemblance to the element of chance deployed by Dadaist practices, in which the "act" of error represents a creative leap in the name of freedom from all determination. Thus, "the forces within man enter into a relation with forces from the outside, those of silicon which supersedes carbon, or genetic components which supersede the organism, or agrammaticalities which supersede the signifier."[18]

And yet can we accept this parallelism at all? Life = Dada? That is, can we accept this Dadaesque image of the powers of chance as the most singular creation of Life itself, or is this what Foucault intended by referring to the singular manner that life has invented, in the form of man, to carry within itself the eventuality of error? Just as the "errors of Life itself" cannot be understood within a closed system of determinations, the powers accorded to chance can no longer be represented by a traditional and humanist concept of freedom as in the case of the above formulation. Consequently, if only for this reason, most of what Deleuze portrays here under the principle of Mallarméan chance must be regarded as nostalgically Romantic – did not Romanticism fundamentally invest life (or nature) with a creative capacity of error in the figure of the sublime, and is this not also another chapter in the history of biopower? Finally, it is for the same reason that I have also understood what Deleuze wrote just a year later in describing a "Society of Control" as only another, perhaps darker, version of the same principle of "unlimited infinity" evoking every situation of force where a finite number of components yields a practically "unlimited diversity of combinations," in which the idea of Control would simply be the "Superfold" of power relations pertaining to the expansion of late capitalist societies.

Nevertheless, and so as not to throw the baby out with the bathwater, I find compelling Deleuze's definition of Man as essentially a "deterritorialized animal," in charge not only of the codes of language, "but also of animals and whatever is yet unformed," in accord with the famous remark by Rimbaud.[19] In my view this is perhaps the most non-Aristotelian definition of animality that exists in contemporary philosophy, and there is something extremely productive in the definition of the eventuality of error as a "point of deterritorialization" that is virtual in any finite combination of forces, including the form of Man, as long as this virtuality is not assigned any immediate moral value. For example, in what way can we say that the new forms of chance and anomaly introduced by the forms of modern art, or the agrammaticalities explored in certain literary works, did not have a relation to the manner in which chance and anomaly evolve in more complex living and informational systems? And did not Dada present this aspect in drawing the chaos of chance encounters into its compositions and turning these sudden chances into elements of signification (i.e., new "percepts" and "affects")? What is called style in art is a simple act that first appears as error, or as anomaly, until it is obsessively repeated and gradually achieves the form of a coherent figure. As Deleuze and Guattari will later state, the modern artwork draws up a little bit of chaos and places it into its frame to create a composed chaos, or a *chaosmos*. But where does the artist derive this element of chaos except from the other systems that occupy its immediate milieu, perhaps in the manner that Foucault discovered in a writer like Roussel, and Deleuze in his stable of writers such as Artaud, Carroll, Péguy, Burroughs, Cummings, to name several?[20] Moreover, this also corresponds to Foucault's own prescription that the forms of chance and error belonging to other systems should be incorporated into the history of truth, and that "the entire theory of the subject would have to be reformulated once knowledge, instead of opening to the truth of the world, is rooted in the 'errors of life'."[21] Consequently, similar to what happened with Foucault's concept of "biopower," it is significant that the collective analysis of the new materialism is today following Foucault's prescription that the form of error expressed in other ontological regions be incorporated into the philosophical narrative of truth, even though this inheritance and influence is never acknowledged as such, according to the precept that "no dominant hero today strides along the beach."[22]

Therefore, if the eventuality of error is considered as an "act" that is virtual in any system of possibilities, then the task of both the historian of science and the philosopher would be the reconstruction of the theoretical, technical, and epistemo-logical conditions in order to account for the visibility of certain objects (or, as in this case, of life), or in simpler terms, quoting Canguilhem, "to cause to be that which is not."[23] But this leads me to a final question: *In what manner can the concept of life be understood as simply an element of signification?* In response, following Canguilhem's earlier insight, this can only occur in the reduction of life, or "Life itself," to the living, since it is only from the perspective of the living being (whether at the level of the individual organism or the single cell) that the appearance of Life itself becomes an element of signification, and it is only from the perspective of the living being that life becomes a reflective matter, the expression of the individual in its *resistance* to that which it is not.[24] Perhaps in a manner that also recalls Duns Scotus' earlier definition of a *Haecceity*, the individual is defined in terms of the "minimum of being" necessary in order for it to express its own principle of individuation. However, contrary to the medieval notion, this limit of divisibility is not to be understood as an essence that belongs to the organism, but rather as a frontier between being and non-being that constantly traverses the organism and places it in touch with its milieu, its environment, and constitutes its very relationally to other beings, both organic and inorganic. Therefore, as in proposition IV of Spinoza's *Ethics*, the individual is defined as a relation to both a greater force, which surpasses it, and a lesser force, which it includes, and thus is always in a state of perpetual discontinuity with itself. Perhaps error would simply be another name for this radical principle of discontinuity in being, and "Life itself" simply the capacity to err, to never be found in one's own place, which is expressed to a greater degree in some living systems than in others, including "the form of Man" (Foucault). Consequently, perhaps it is fitting that I conclude my investigation where I began: simply by calling our attention to the fact that these last reflections of Foucault on "the errors of life" were made with the full knowledge of the anomalies that were traversing his own body, and that would soon culminate at a threshold where the individual finally succumbs to the limit of non-being through the very error of Life itself.

Notes

1   Nietzsche, *The Gay Science*, p. 101.
2   Foucault, *Dits et écrits*, vol. 2, p. 1585.
3   Ibid.

4 Bergson, *An Introduction to Metaphysics*, p. 168.

5 Foucault, *Archeology of Knowledge*, p. 49.

6 Bergson, *An Introduction to Metaphysics*, p. 11.

7 Ibid. The original French reads: "À toute affirmation vraie nous attribuons ainsi un effet rétroactif, ou plutôt nous lui imprimons un mouvement retrograde."

8 Lacan, *The Ego in Freud's Theory and in the Technique of Psychoanalysis*, p. 49.

9 Ibid.

10 Ibid.

11 Foucault, *Dits et écrits*, vol. 2, p. 1593.

12 Ibid., pp. 1593–4.

13 Ibid.

14 Ibid.

15 Deleuze, *Foucault*, p. 130.

16 Ibid.

17 Ibid., p. 131.

18 Ibid., pp. 130–1.

19 Ibid., p. 153, n. 18.

20 Of course, this stable would need to be enlarged and populated by many other writers like Perec who have explored the limits of the formal and combinatory possibilities of life and error.

21 Foucault, *Dits et écrits*, vol. 2, p. 1594.

22 This is the statement of *kudos* announced in the opening of the collection *The Speculative Turn*:

> No dominant hero now strides along the beach, as the phase of subservient commentary on the history of philosophy seems to have ended. Genuine attempts at full-blown systematic thought are no longer rare in our circles; increasingly, they are even expected. And whatever the possible drawbacks of globalization, the new global networks have worked very much in our favour: enhanced technologies have made the blogosphere and online booksellers major contributors to a new "primordial soup" of continental philosophy. Though it is too early to know what strange life forms might evolve from this mixture, it seems clear enough that something important is happening. In our profession, there has never been a better time to be young (Bryant et al., *The Speculative Turn*, p. 1).

23 "La Concept de la vie," in Canguilhem, *Etudes de histoire et de philosophie des sciences concernait les vivants et la vie*, p. 343. See also Cutro, *Techique et vie: biopolitique et philosophie le pensée de Michel Foucault*.

24 "The individual is a being at the limit of non-being, being that which cannot be fragmented further without losing its proper characteristics that define it as an individual being." Canguilhem, "Cellular Theory," in *Knowledge of Life*, p. 70. See also ibid., p. 128.

Bibliography

Alain Badiou, *Ethics: An Essay on the Understanding of Evil*, trans. Peter Hallward, London: Verso, 2002.

Roland Barthes, *Mythologies*, New York: Noonday Press, 1972.

— *Saint Paul: The Foundation of Universalism*, trans. Ray Brassier, Stanford: Stanford University Press, 2003.

Georges Bataille, *Absence of Myth: Writings on Surrealism*, trans. Michael Richardson, London: Verso, 1994.

— *On Nietzsche*, London: Continuum, 2000.

Emile Benveniste, *Le Vocabulaire des institutions indo-Europeennes, tome 2 (pouvoir, droit, religion)*, Paris: Minuit, 1969.

Henri Bergson, *An Introduction to Metaphysics*, trans. T. E. Hulme, New York and London: Putnam & Sons, 1912.

— *Two Sources of Religion and Morality*, London: Macmillan, 1935.

Maurice Blanchot, *The Inavowable Community*, trans. Pierre Joris, New York: Station Hill Press, 1988.

Levi Bryant, et al. (eds), *The Speculative Turn: Continental Materialism and Realism*, Melbourne: re.press, 2011.

Judith Butler, *Bodies That Matter*, London: Routledge, 1993.

Georges Canguilhem, *Etudes de histoire et de philosophie des sciences concernait les vivants et la vie*, Paris: Vrin, 1994.

— *Knowledge of Life*, ed. Paolo Marrati and Todd Meyers, trans. Stefanos Geroulanos and Daniela Ginsburg, New York: Fordham University Press, 2008.

John D. Caputo, *Against Ethics: Contributions to a Poetics of Obligation with Constant Reference to Deconstruction*, Bloomington: Indiana University Press, 1993.

— *The Prayers and Tears of Jacques Derrida*, Bloomington: Indiana University Press, 1997.

— *On Religion*, New York: Routledge, 2001.

— "Love Among Deconstructibles," *Journal of Cultural and Religious Theory* (April 2004).

— *Philosophy and Theology*, Nashville: Abingdon Press, 2006.

— *The Weakness of God: A Theology of the Event*, Bloomington: Indiana University Press, 2006.

Antonella Cutro, *Téchique et vie: biopolitique et philosophie le pensée de Michel Foucault*, Paris: Harmattan, 2010.

Gilles Deleuze, *Foucault*, trans. Sean Hand, Minneapolis: University of Minnesota Press, 1988.

Gilles Deleuze and Félix Guattari, *A Thousand Plateaus: Capitalism and Schizophrenia*, vol. 2, trans. Brian Massumi, Minneapolis: University of Minnesota Press, 1987.

Jacques Derrida, "Fors," in Nicolas Abraham and Maria Torok, *The Wolf Man's Magic Word: A Cryptonomy*, trans. Nicholas Rand, Minneapolis: University of Minnesota Press, 1986, pp. xi–il.

— *Le Toucher: Jean-Luc Nancy*, Paris: Galilée, 2000.

— *Acts of Religion*, London: Routledge, 2002.

— *On Touching: Jean-Luc Nancy*, trans. Christine Izarray, Stanford: Stanford University Press, 2005.

— *The Beast and the Sovereign*, vol. 1, trans. Geoffrey Bennington, Chicago: University of Chicago Press, 2009.

— *Perjury and Pardon*, vol. 1, trans. David Wills, Chicago: University of Chicago Press, forthcoming 2016.

— and Gianni Vattimo, *Religion*, Stanford: Stanford University Press, 1998.

Patrick ffrench, *After Bataille: Sacrifice, Exposure, Community*, London: Legenda, 2007.

Michel Foucault, "What is Enlightenment?" in *The Foucault Reader*, ed. Paul Rabinow, New York: Pantheon Books, 1984.

— *Dits et écrits*, vol. 2 (1976–88), Paris: Gallimard, 1994.

— *The Archeology of Knowledge*, London: Routledge, 2002.

Sigmund Freud, *Beyond the Pleasure Principle*, *Complete Psychological Works*, vol. 18, New York: W. W. Norton, 2001.

— *Civilization and its Discontents*, ed. Peter Gay, New York: W. W. Norton, 1989.

Wlad Godzich, "Introduction: Caution! Reader at Work!," in Paul de Man, *Blindness and Insight: Essays in the Rhetoric of Contemporary Criticism*, Minneapolis: University of Minnesota Press, 1983, pp. xv–xxx.

Garret Green, "Modern Culture Comes of Age: Hamann versus Kant on the Root Metaphor of the Enlightenment," in James Schmidt (ed.), *What is Enlightenment? Eighteenth-Century Answers and Twentieth-Century Questions*, Berkeley: University of California Press, 1996.

Martin Hägglund, *Radical Atheism: Derrida and the Time of Life*, Stanford: Stanford University Press, 2008.

Martin Heidegger, *Question Concerning Technology and Other Essays*, trans. William Lovitt, New York: Harper & Rowe, 1977.

— *Pathmarks*, trans. William McNeil, Cambridge: Cambridge University Press, 1998.

— *The Phenomenology of Religious Life*, trans. Matthias Fritsch and Jennifer Anna Gosetti-Ferencei, Bloomington: Indiana University Press, 2010.

Denis Hollier, *Le College de Sociologie: 1937–1939*, Paris: Gallimard, 1955.

— *College of Sociology*, trans. Betsy Wing, Minneapolis: University of Minnesota Press, 1988.

Max Horkheimer, "Reason Against Itself: Some Remarks on Enlightenment," in James Schmidt (ed.), *What is Enlightenment? Eighteenth-Century Answers and Twentieth-Century Questions*, Berkeley: University of California Press, 1996.

Fredric Jameson, "How Not to Historicize Theory," *Critical Inquiry* 34 (2008), pp. 563–82.

Dominique Janicaud et al., *Phenomenology and the "Theological Turn,"* New York: Fordham University Press, 2000.

Immanuel Kant, "Beantwortung der Frage: Was ist Auklärung?," *Berlinische Monatsschrift*, 1st edn Berlin: J. F. Unger, 1793.

Peter Klein, "Skepticism," *The Stanford Encyclopedia of Philosophy* (Summer 2015 Edition), ed. Edward N. Zalta, at <http://plato.stanford.edu/archives/sum2015/entries/skepticism/> (accessed 21 October 2015).

Thomas Kuhn, *The Structure of Scientific Revolutions*, Chicago: Chicago University Press, 1996.

Jacques Lacan, *The Ego in Freud's Theory and in the Technique of Psychoanalysis*, trans. Sylvana Tomaselli, Cambridge: Cambridge University Press, 1988.

— *Four Fundamental Concepts of Psychoanalysis*, ed. Jacques-Alain Miller, trans. Alan Sheridan, New York: W. W. Norton, 1998.

— *On Feminine Sexuality, the Limits of Love and Knowledge (Encore)*, ed. Jacques-Alain Miller, trans. Bruce Fink, New York: W. W. Norton, 1999.

Jean Laplanche and J. B. Pontalis, *The Language of Psychoanalysis.* New York: W. W. Norton, 1974.

Emmanuel Levinas, *Humanisme de l'autre homme*, Paris: Fata Morgana, 1972.

— *Existence and Existents*, trans. Alphonos Lingis, The Hague: Martinus Nijhoff, 1978.

Wayne A. Meeks, "Since Then You Would Need to go Out Into the World: Group Boundaries in Early Christianity," in T. J. Ryan (ed.), *Critical History and Biblical Perspective*, Villanova: College Theology Society, 1979.

— *The First Urban Christians: The Social World of the Apostle Paul*, New Haven: Yale University Press, 1983.

Michael Naas, *Miracle and Machine: Jacques Derrida and the Two Sources of Religion, Science, and the Media*, New York: Fordham University Press, 2012.

Jean-Luc Nancy, *The Inoperative Community*, trans. Peter Connor, Minneapolis: University of Minnesota Press, 1991.

— *Being Singular Plural*, trans. Robert D. Richardson et al., Stanford: Stanford University Press, 2000.

— *Corpus*, Paris: Editions Metailie, 2000.

— *La Communauté affrontée*, Paris: Galilée, 2001.

— *Dis-enclosure: The Deconstruction of Christianity*, trans. Bettina Bergo et al., New York: Fordham University Press, 2008.

— and Philip Armstrong and Jason Smith *Politique et au-delà*, Paris: Galilée, 2011.

Fredrich Nietzsche, *The Gay Science*, ed. Bernard Williams, Cambridge: Cambridge University Press, 2001.

Jean-Paul Sartre, *Being and Nothingness: An Essay on Phenomenological Ontology*, New York: Philosophical Library, 1956.

Elizabeth Schüssler-Fiorenza, *In Memory of Her: Feminist Theological Reconstructions of Christian Origins*, Minneapolis: Fortress, 1983.

Leslie Silko and James Wright, *The Delicacy and Strength of Lace*, ed. Anne Wright, Saint Paul: Graywolf Press, 1986.

Benedictus de Spinoza, *The Ethics: Treatise on the Emendation of the Intellect*, ed. G. H. R. Parkinson, Oxford: Oxford University Press, 2000.

— *Theological-Political Treatise*, 2nd edn, Indianapolis: Hackett Publishing, 2001.

Herman Waetjen, *A Reordering of Power: A Socio-Political Reading of Mark's Gospel*, Minneapolis: Fortress, 1989.

Jack Wiseman, *Beyond Positive Economics*, London: Macmillan, 1983.

Index